MQ410594
7.25
MEDIA

Pictures on the Page

Pictures on the Page

Judith Graham

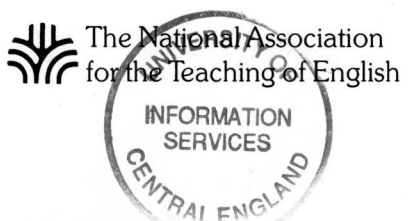

The National Association
for the Teaching of English

Edited for NATE by Liz Grugeon and Dennis Pepper

Design by Dennis Pepper

First published: November 1990

Published by The National Association for the Teaching of English
Birley School Annexe, Fox Lane, Frecheville, Sheffield S12 4WY

ISBN: 0 901291 20 X

First printed in England by Short Run Press Ltd, Exeter

Contents

Judith Graham and NATE are grateful to the artists and their publishers for permission to 'quote' from the books discussed here. Black and white reproductions, often reduced in size, give little indication of the quality of the original illustrations. The reader is urged to consult the books themselves, details of which are given in the bibliography and in the acknowledgements on page 126.

The Way In

From the moment they are born, children in our culture are surrounded not only by reality in the form of people and objects and actions but also by a different sort of reality, representations of reality which issue from television screen and radio, posters, pictures and books. It may take the child some time to work out how this second order reality is related to and reflects upon the first, but there is no doubt that for many children the representation is as intriguing as the real thing.

Visual representations are believed to have been part of human society for almost five thousand years. No doubt children enjoyed jabbing small fingers at paintings of animals on cave walls in much the same way as they touch and stare fixedly at a striped tiger pictured in a board book today. Apart from toys, which stand half-way between the real world and the symbolic world, pictures seem to be the easiest symbolic form for children to grasp. They communicate easily compared with more arbitrary 'signifiers' such as words because they represent the appearance of the 'signified' more exactly. There is some dispute on the question of how much we have to learn to read pictorial representations. Clearly a highly conventionalized picture, let us say a late Picasso portrait, is harder to 'read' than a realistic likeness but even in the most 'natural' photograph some distortion, selection and transformation has taken place. Nevertheless, for most children it seems that a short time is needed to adjust to any difference between how they see objects in reality and how they see them in pictures.

Assuming that cultural ways of seeing are shared and that visual representations are common in a society, children normally are attracted by images which reflect both their immediate world and unknown worlds to them. We bind these various pictures into board books where the image holds still and can be closely and repeatedly inspected. From there it is a short step for our pedagogic natures to put a label or caption below the picture and trust that the repeated labelling games will enable the intent eye of the child to pick up the more complex symbolic system of language. Researchers such as Diane Schallert (1980) dissent from this view: 'Because pictures can already elicit an appropriate verbal response they interfere with the beginning reader's ability to concentrate on and learn to discriminate properly the printed stimuli'. The view of the reading process that this belief rests on will be looked at in Chapter 1. However, parents and teachers are usually well aware of how an illustration triggers memory of the text and of how 'reading-like behaviour' can quickly become real reading. Picture-books which add narrative continue the seduction of the child and hence we have the easily accessible, possibly educational and spell-binding artifact that flourishes in our society today. With its wide, identifiable and enthusiastic audience, adults as well as children, the picture-book attracts many gifted authors and illustrators. Vastly improved printing techniques, the impact of twentieth century art movements, the influence of television and graphic design and more enlightened educational attitudes have all had a share in the development of the picture-book as the child's most important aesthetic and educational object.

However, there is one important respect in which the picture-book has been underestimated. The illustrations obviously attract and delight; what has been very much overlooked or at any rate taken for granted is the part that the illustrations in a picture-book may play in the literary development of a reader. Always the general assumption has been that the pictures lure the child into the book and that once there attention to the language will develop reading abilities. Of course, this is not unlikely and I would not want to deny the power of a good narrative text to contribute to the development of readers. But I shall be arguing that we must not ignore the potential in the illustration of a book to create readers, not only in their own right as in a wordless text, but also when combined in certain telling ways with a carefully constructed text. Illustrations are thus very much more than 'cobwebs to catch flies' as they have been called.

It is perhaps not surprising that the contribution of illustrations to reading development has been seriously underestimated. It is only relatively recently that our understanding of the reading process has broadened sufficiently for us to recognize that anything other than close attention to letters was what mattered. How our understanding of the act of reading has grown for it to include such matters as knowledge of narrative conventions and 'imaging' (or interior visualization) is the subject of the first two chapters. How illustrations make their contribution to these and other growing competences in the developing reader is investigated in the remainder of this study.

A quick glance at the bibliography might suggest that illustration in children's books gives rise, if not to many full-length books, then at least to a healthy number of serious articles both here and in the United States. Journals such as *Signal, Children's Literature in Education, Books for Keeps* and the *Horn Book Magazine* have paid increasing attention to picture-books and the arts/humanities journal *Word and Image* has devoted a whole issue to children's art and literature. Elaine Moss in her campaign to widen the audience for picture-books has done much to raise the status of the genre and both Jill Bennett and the Inner London Education Authority have produced important guides to picture-books.

Unfortunately, the myriad problems which beset the criticism of children's literature do not disappear when the genre under discussion is picture-books. The book-centred approach still vies with the child-centred approach, the literary-critical with the sociological, the historical with the psychological. The addition of illustrations is often one further headache for critics to contend with as many feel they do not have a language with which to describe and assess the pictures and so may ignore the illustrations or refer to them parenthetically. This incurs the wrath of an illustrator such as Celia Berridge (1981) who argues that picture-books are judged far too much as 'works of literature, and not nearly enough as works of visual art'. I feel her prescription would be equally unsatisfactory and in particular her 'personal response' method of book evaluation ('I trust my own taste absolutely') offers no real philosophy to anyone undertaking an assessment of the role of the picture-book in a child's reading life. An expert reviewer such as Jane Doonan, who is both art historian and Head of an English Department, is rare in the field, but even her interest is not in the role of illustration in early literacy. Brian Wildsmith's books she feels (1986A) are 'invitations to a child to reach for a *brush*' (my italics) and her excellent detailed review of *Granpa* still has to be supplemented by Nancy Chambers' editorial comment in order to include the reader response. (*Signal*, 1985)

So whilst I am indebted to the insights offered by those whose work is listed in the bibliography, because my aim is to explore the relationship of the picture-book to early literacy, I have in fact had to evolve a way of my own to approach the assessment of the books discussed. With each book I have tried to answer the questions – could these illustrations initiate children into the conventions of narrative? Could this picture-book play a formative role in the making of a reader? To my knowledge, no one approaches the picture-book in order to isolate what narrative conventions the illustrations teach. Many of us have for some time pleaded for the relationship between children's literature and theories of literacy to be further explored. The present study is my contribution to that exploration.

1. The Act of Reading

> But first I eagerly scanned what text there was in the middle, in order to get a hint of what it was all about. Of course I was not going to waste any time in reading. A clue, a sign-board, a finger-post was all I required. To my dismay and disgust it was all in a stupid foreign language! Really, the perversity of some people made one at times almost despair of the whole race. However, the pictures remained; pictures never lied, never shuffled nor evaded; and as for the story, I could invent it myself.
>
> Kenneth Grahame, 1898

When I first began teaching in the early sixties, children who couldn't read were streamed out of my classes and I taught those who were left in the way I myself had been taught, in the best 'Eng. Lit.' tradition. There was much reading aloud of key moments and a great deal of setting of homework on plot, character and themes. How children made sense of the print in their texts and what constituted their literary literacy was not investigated. By the late sixties I started helping individual children with their reading and although I sensed its inadequacies, the very powerful behaviourist view of what reading involves undoubtedly shaped my teaching and restricted my thinking. For a young practising teacher there was little known alternative to the view that reading involved first, 'making a discriminatory response to graphic symbols (word and letter recognition; decoding)'; secondly, 'encoding the graphic symbol into speech (sound symbol association)'; and thirdly, 'getting meaning through the arousal of associative material via memory traces and schemata.' (Joan Hart & G. A. Richardson, 1971). The fact that the above views could be found in a vast number of books on the subject of reading before 1971 and a considerable number since indicates the dominance exerted by this narrow view of reading, developed first in the 1920s in an attempt to establish behaviour on a scientific basis rather than the earlier, more philosophical, humanist approach. Along with this view went specific pedagogic practices which stressed learning by rote, practice, repetition, imitation, habit formation, association and other favourite behaviourist practices, all directed towards what we now call the sub-skills of reading. The saddest aspect of the power this view had is that it inhibited our best instincts of how to help children become readers, prevented our sharing our literary competences or noticing those of our pupils, and drove a wedge between learning to read and reading.

In my classroom in those early days, eleven-year-old James was reading *The Giant Alexander* (Methuen) to me. We had learnt that the giant, as tall as two telegraph poles, lived by the sea in Maldon, Essex. He was visited at breakfast time by the coastguard requesting help for a ship stuck on a sandbank. The giant 'wiped his beard with a red tablecloth' and set off to help. James cheerfully read that the giant whipped his bread with a red tablecloth. I waited with interest to see if this miscue would be corrected but he pressed on. In the event, I have much to thank him for because that small miscue has revealed much over the years about the act of reading.

Under the influence of a sub-skills model, I might have instituted a programme of exercises with James practising 'wh' sounds and 'br' blends and if he hadn't been very good at putting this piece of learning into practice, I might have begun to let the word dyslexia flit through my mind. But what is in fact going on here? James is obviously a dab hand at grammar. In Chomsky's terms, there are no problems here with his knowledge of deep grammatical structures – nouns and verbs are all in the right places, tenses are sorted out and he knows all about subject – verb – object word order. Like all of us, if he'd upset the grammatical integrity of the sentence, he would probably have recast the whole sentence in order to get back to a syntactic fit. This in fact happened when later he read "The trouble is my boots are being repaired" as "The trouble with my boots is that they are being repaired". Having inserted 'with', there had to be further insertions to avoid a syntactic confusion.

With this second miscue, James preserved meaning, as in fact all fluent readers tend to. It could reasonably be argued that "whipped his bread" strays a long way from the author's intended message and that, however healthy on a syntactic level, it comes close to a wild guess on a semantic level. It was

Kenneth Goodman (1969) who likened the act of reading to a 'psycho-linguistic guessing game', but he was not referring to wild guesses. His definition relates to how we use our knowledge of language and of our life experiences to read off the text quickly, sampling it to confirm our informed predictions of what it contains.

Now in life, we don't usually go around whipping loaves of bread with tablecloths. James's prediction of the text at this point was not rooted in his first-hand experience of life. However his miscue could be related to the expectations he has of stories and especially stories about giants where perhaps anything can happen. The fact that this bizarre behaviour is in the event *not* characteristic of this particular giant becomes clear as the story develops and, if all systems were operating, we would want James to reflect at some point and query that early eccentricity of the giant. In doing so, he would undoubtedly correct his miscue.

Looked at in this light, the miscue becomes evidence that this boy is an inexperienced reader who needs to know more about how stories go so that he may question the text and self-correct at ever earlier stages. Revision would then become as immediate as it is with fluent readers. The confidence needed to self-correct is obviously a feature of experience and a sign of feeling safe.

This analysis of the act of reading so far indicates that it is very far from a mechanical un-picking of the written code and relies much more on what is in our heads already in terms of knowledge about language and life. In real life, we are able to anticipate likely events from what has gone before, to draw inferences, to develop ideas logically, to use context clues, to make something meaningful of events around us. So it is with reading.

The act of reading also depends upon other competences that we have developed as we grow up or that are perhaps innate. Barbara Hardy (1968, in Meek, Warlow and Barton 1977) throws light on the all-pervasive presence of narrative in our lives. She argues that narrative 'is not to be regarded as an aesthetic invention used by artists to control, manipulate and order experience, but as a primary act of mind transferred to art from life.' The novel, she claims, 'merely heightens, isolates and analyses the narrative motions of human consciousness.' This central role given to narrative does not preclude our need to learn the narrative conventions that writers use. Culler (1978) insists that literary competences must be made explicit and taught. 'Literary works may be quite baffling to those with no knowledge of the special conventions of literary discourse.' James, as dependent upon and competent at storytelling as the rest of his class, needed more acquaintance with the patterns and shapes of stories which are traditionally found in books in our society. How picture-books contribute to the learning of these literary conventions is the focus of this study.

Deepening our understanding of the act of reading still further, D. W. Harding (1962, in Meek, Warlow and Barton 1977) gives us the idea of the reader taking an 'active part at the receiving end of a conventional mode of communication' in contrast with the view of fiction reading as one of identification or vicarious experience. This theory of active reader participation finds its fullest description in the work of Wolfgang Iser. The 'unsaid' (the telling gaps or blanks) in a work of fiction is filled by the reader and in the process the 'said' expands and triggers reflections in the reader. The reader's activity is still controlled by the text but the reader 'sets the work in motion and becomes a kind of co-author' (1978). Authors, it appears, really need readers to complete the realization of their texts. This emphasis on the active role of the reader (which needs to be understood and modelled by parents and teachers) further accentuates the restricted horizons of the view of reading as decoding, encoding and getting meaning. We shall see how picture-books depend upon, teach and reward active participation in their readers.

Finally, and briefly, we need to see how the act of reading depends for its success upon two other inter-related points. Tolkien (1964) helped us to see that one of the things a reader has to do is to be willing to enter a secondary world. Whilst you are 'in' the secondary world you believe it; if disbelief arises, the spell is broken. That children create a secondary world with its own rules whilst they are playing should encourage us to see what play and stories have in common. Are books the best game of all? And we need also to know that the act of reading has its roots in feeling. James Britton (1970) advocates stories of witches and fairy godmothers ('images that clothe inner instinctual needs') and the evidence we have that children read and re-read such books as *Not now, Ber-*

nard (David McKee), where the substitution of child by monster goes unnoticed by the parents, suggests that emotional engagement is central to the process.

James's experience of books was limited. His history did not necessarily make it easier for him to build up mutual meanings with authors; it may have been too much of a risk for him to surrender to the secondary world created by the book; he may not have had as much opportunity of symbolic play as he should have done. But in many ways he had important bits of the jigsaw puzzle together. What might have helped, perhaps even at this late stage, would have been more immersion in picture-books, where some of the complex lessons of reading are taught. Before we look at picture-books in detail we need to inspect one further element of the reading process, the act of 'picturing' or 'visualization'.

2. The Act of Picturing

"In my mind I can see the forest with the bear coming tramping through it . . . I think I could draw what I saw".

Donald Fry, 1985

"Now I'm picturing big black skies, black as a cloak they used to wear in the olden days. I just pictured that, blacking out the sky; and there's the forest which seems very, very small . . . and the lightning seems to me, well, in the picture in my mind, it seems bigger than normal lightning. I don't know why, it's just a picture in my mind".

Michael Benton and Geoff Fox, 1985

These two young readers are reflecting on the picturing or imaging that occurs during the reading process. Donald Fry writes of picturing as a 'fundamental act of imagining by the reader necessary to make sense of what is read' and Michael Benton (1979) claims that 'the images stimulated by the text are the carriers of information about the Secondary World to the brain and correspond to the functions of the five senses in our perception of the Primary World'. He and Geoff Fox conclude that picturing is 'the most important element in the way in which a reader brings a story to imaginative life'. Many readers may claim that they experience little picturing when reading or are only dimly aware of its operations or by-pass the picturing state, going straight to abstractions, but it is likely that, 'pictures and stories (being) the mind's stock-in-trade' (Susanne Langer, 1953), it is a universal process.

We may well wonder where these pictures come from. Michael Benton learns from one boy that the composite image he has of the lakeside in *Swallows and Amazons* springs from the boy's visit to Lake Coniston three months earlier, details from the West Coast of Scotland from four years prior to that and yet more details from Arthur Ransome's frontispiece map. Whether it is always possible to unravel these influences I doubt: we may want to agree with Tolkien (1964) that 'every hearer of the words will have his own picture, and it will be made out of all the hills and rivers and dales he has ever seen, but especially out of The Hill, The River, The Valley which were for him the first embodiment of the word'.

In this chapter I want to explore the relationship between picturing and pictures, specifically between picturing and the illustrations that are so much a part of children's early experience of books at least in our culture. It is problematic because we have Bruno Bettelheim (1976) declaring, 'Illustrated story books . . . do not serve the child's best needs. The illustrations are distracting rather than helpful. Studies of illustrated primers demonstrate that the pictures divert from the learning process rather than foster it because the illustrations direct the child's imagination away from how he, on his own, would experience the story. The illustrated story is robbed of much content of personal meaning which it could bring to the child who applied only his own visual association to the story, instead of those of the illustrator.' It is not that Bettelheim questions that we picture as we read: indeed he places such emphasis on this aspect of the process that he wants nothing to interfere with it and he points a finger at illustrations in books as obstructive and impoverishing. Tolkien also claims that 'however good in themselves, illustrations do little to fairy stories'.

Taken to a logical conclusion these severe statements might indicate that far from being stepping-stones into the world of reading picture-books are preventing children from bringing their own images and meanings to the story and so are denying them the full reading experience. Shirley Hughes (1985) has confessed to being troubled by this issue – 'I hope I'm not doing myself out of a job if I say that the best pictures any child sees are in its own head. That power of interior visualization is one of the most amazing of human attributes.' She goes on to say that she has no idea where these pictures come from. I would like to say that a possible source is those very illustrations that Bettelheim so condemns.

One hopes that Bettleheim and Tolkien would not dismiss some of the newer picture-books such as *Rosie's Walk, Where the Wild Things Are, Come away from the water, Shirley* and many others which I shall be discussing later where so interwoven with the text are the pictures that to give the text alone would be like giving a performance of a concerto without an orchestra. Text and illustrations in books such as these invite the reader to enter their mutual game.

But what if we turn to a picture-book where the text seems to be able to stand on its own? *John Brown, Rose and the Midnight Cat* has a gentle story by Jenny Wagner of a widow and her dog and their difference of opinion on whether a stray cat should live with them. The text is divided up, two or three lines to a page, in the rather 'old-fashioned' way under illustrations by Ron Brooks. I read this book, withholding the pictures, to various listeners, both adults and children, who either reported a minimum level of picturing ("It's really about a relationship which is pretty abstract", "because it's nearly all in dialogue you don't see them, only hear them") or described what they 'saw' as occurring in their own homes and gardens. Rose is an archetypal old lady and John Brown is a mongrel. The cat is always black ('midnight' in the text).

On turning to the illustrations several interesting points arise. Firstly, Ron Brooks's illustrations are always received as the perfectly valid picturings of another person's imagination. "Yes, it could be like that. Rose could wear glasses on the end of her nose and wear slippers all the time. John Brown could be a shaggy sheepdog, their home could be a curious wooden construction with a Victorian feel to the interior." Most reported that Brooks's illustrations expanded their own very much more stereotypical homespun images. But it became very apparent that readers were meeting Brooks's images half way: readers' heads are not empty of images when they open a picture-book any more than they are empty of ideas when they open a text. Pictures, like words, mean because readers bring meaning to them. Kay Chorao (1979) speaks of a child's interpretation of illustrations being unique and 'shaped by his own point of view not the artist's. Children filter art as they do all life experiences through their own perspectives'.

Secondly, and most excitingly, readers began to explore divergences between their pictures and those of the artist. "I didn't see the dog as big as that. I didn't see the dog cuddling her, sitting in what is obviously her late husband's chair, sitting up to table, pulling the curtains shut. He seems to be a husband substitute. And isn't he wilful? *My* John Brown was merely indifferent to Rose's enthusiasm: Ron Brooks's dog positively sabotages her schemes." And finally, readers comment on the cat. "It wasn't until I saw the pictures of the cat that I realized the story could be about something other than the dog's possessiveness. *My* cat was fairly harmless and only

'We are all right, John Brown,' said Rose.
'Just the two of us, you and me.'

Jenny Wagner &
Ron Brooks
*John Brown, Rose
and the Midnight Cat*

important as an object of Rose's generous attitude to animals. In Brooks's pictures the cat has a far more insistent quality – unnerving really, could she be a symbol of death?'' It is interesting to discover that when Ron Brooks first submitted his illustrations for this text John Brown, the dog, was depicted on his hind legs throughout wearing Rose's late husband's clothes and smoking his pipe. The end papers depicted tombstones. Clearly his editor realized that 'telling gaps'

One night Rose looked out of the window
and saw something move in the garden.

needed to be left for the reader to work at in illustrations as
well as words and advised against these too literal early ver-
sions.

Readers thus seemed to be saying that it was only through
Ron Brooks's illustrations that they were enabled to
appreciate the fine distinction drawn between loyalty and
jealousy, to perceive the dangers of assuming proprietorship,
to ponder on whether the cat symbolized death or feminine

'What's that in the garden, John Brown?' she said.
John Brown would not look.

solidarity (without the cat to strengthen her John Brown will
deny Rose all liveliness and incident). Very experienced readers may bring all these meanings to the text alone; for the
young readers I worked with there was no doubt that the
addition of the illustrations gave access to deeper levels of
meaning-making. A class of eight- and nine-year-olds with
whom I shared the book were able to form some of these
understandings and frequently referred to such details as John

Brown's paw resting poignantly on Rose's slipper as he wrestles with his jealousy or to the vast emptiness of the double bed and the numerous photographs of Rose's late husband which emphasize mortality.

Have we then in fact examined a picture-book that belongs, after all, with the books listed earlier where no subtracting of the illustrations is possible? Certainly the limited review of this book which Bob Dixon (1982) gives calling it 'sex-stereotyped' and 'obnoxious' suggests he failed to see how the illustrations were extending the text. I think the text is just suggestive enough to enable experienced readers to expand its implications themselves; certainly the mood of anxiety and threat, the themes of love and fear are present in the text alone but for inexperienced readers there is no doubt that the illustrations set these moods and unlock these themes whilst also enlarging and enhancing their growing stock of visual representations.

I needed to examine what the effect of illustration would be on readers' picturing processes if a text which had clearly been successful in an un-illustrated form for several decades were put to the test. I turned to Charles Keeping's illustrations for Alfred Noyes's *The Highwayman*. A quick recall of the poem and a glance at Keeping's illustrations reminds us that this is not a book for the youngest readers. Inevitably I would have to work with older students at secondary school or beyond, but I was still trying to ascertain what impact powerful illustrations would have on a listener/reader's own images.

With this text, at first heard only, there was no by-passing the picturing process. The text of course invites imaging:

> He'd a French cocked-hat on his forehead, a bunch of lace
>   at his chin.
> A coat of claret velvet and breeches of brown doe-skin.

and many hearers also claimed to 'hear' the 'tlot-tlot in the distance' and 'the clattering and clashing in the dark inn-yard', to 'smell' the 'black cascade of perfumed hair,' to 'feel' the 'coldness of the musket's trigger.' The charged sensuality of the poem is both the source of its appeal to young people and the object of criticism amongst more sophisticated readers but it is not my intention to make a literary evaluation of the poem here; I wanted to use this text because it is clearly a powerfully evocative poem.

They said no word to the landlord. They drank his ale instead.

Alfred Noyes &
Charles Keeping
The Highwayman

A full range of images was reported. For a listener whose childhood was spent in the West Indies, 'the ribbon of moonlight over the purple moor' was a country road back home, the 'gusty trees' in full and exotic leaf. Many commented on the colour in their 'own' pictures, especially red and purple. Many conveyed the sense of being 'dark watchers' (Geoff Fox's phrase). "Sometimes I move in a flash from beside Bess as she pulls the trigger to next to the highwayman. Now I'm looking at his face and his expression; his clothes are unimportant." Many spoke as if describing a film: positioning was important, movement, even of the bullet, was mentioned and the speeding up of various scenes.

On being shown Keeping's illustrations, a clear testing of his vision against their own took place. "Yes, he's got his clothes right", "No, her hair was much longer than that – more like Rapunzel's", and, particularly revealing, "Charles Keeping must have seen the Red Coats' faces. I never saw them but I knew they were threatening." The particularly explicit images of the gagging, tying up and death of Bess (which Keeping defended as a legitimate response to a violent story – *Books for Keeps* No. 16, Sept. 1982) elicited little verbal response although and probably because many found them shocking. Some said later that Keeping's illustrations had ousted their own though one girl said passionately, "How can any illustration match my own pictures? Mine move, mine are in 3D, my highwayman's clothes have texture and warmth, his blood has colour and it runs before my eyes." But generally the verdict was "I could retrieve my own images, but his are easier to recall because, I suppose, they're much better."

Another group met poem and illustrations together. It was clearly more difficult for them to find their own images though several realized that they were bringing images from film and television (and other picture-books?) to aid the creation of meaning. Once Keeping's images are associated with the words of the poem it is probably very difficult and unnecessary to seek another combination of verbal and visual image. This is the situation which troubled Bettelheim. Some of the group were much less enthusiastic about both poem and illustrations, which suggests that both the active role of visualization and the gratifying comparative work of the other group had been denied them.

This appears to lend some weight to Bettelheim and Tolkien's point. However three cautionary notes need to be sounded. Firstly, in choosing *The Highwayman* for this investigation I have considered a text which, because of its highly charged language, is much less in need of powerful illustrations than a text which either because it is simpler or because it leaves much unsaid, would benefit from extending illustrations. It is perhaps significant that Keeping illustrates *Beowulf* and *The Lady of Shalott* with much more suggestive, less literal pictures which leave both texts much more open. Secondly, amongst the groups with whom I read *The Highwayman* there were naturally many readers already adept at their own picturing and thus able to dispense with illustrations to text. And thirdly and conversely, there were also many still so inexperienced as readers that they found Keeping's illustrations a valuable support for their own rather weaker imagining powers. Surely it is the older, struggling reader who is Keeping's 'implied reader' for this book. The conclusion must be tentative, but it suggests that readers know when they are ready to dispense with illustrations and equally they may know when they are still in need of building up their store of visual representations.

There may still be some problems in accepting that the ability to visualize can be fed by picture-books at formative times. People throughout the ages and throughout the world have become literate without picture-books and of course, blind people have no access to picture-books and yet they become readers. However, a quick survey shows how visual representations have always played a role in story telling whether on the walls of caves, in Buddhist temple friezes, as icons or frescoes, statues or stained-glass windows, in shadow puppet plays or in the picture cloths of itinerant story-tellers. Comenius produced his *Orbis Pictus*, widely believed to be the first printed illustrated book designed for children, in 1657 and countless picture sheets, woodblock prints and chap books have been enjoyed for several centuries in many, though mostly Western, countries. Paulo Freire made extensive use of pictures in his literacy programme with Brazilian peasants. Clearly whilst no-one denies that we take images from real life as well, nevertheless the still image, the icon which stays to be contemplated, has always been powerful. Indeed the outcry from critics of an illustrated book on South Africa *The Child is not Dead* (Haries et al., 1986) was a great deal to do with the fact that harsh black and white photographs do not flicker and fade from memory as television pictures do, but remain to speak their message.

As far as the blind reader is concerned I have to rely on an account given by Craig Werner, a blind lecturer in Children's Literature (1984). His experience suggests that a blind child is able at least in part to partake of a visual image by transformation to other senses; thus Andersen's Red Shoes can be appreciated as shiny or Red Riding Hood's cape as furry; Andersen's tin soldier comes clinking out of his box and the fierceness of the troll in *Three Billy Goats Gruff* is known by his terrible and inhuman voice. Craig admits temporary trouble with witches, dragons and ogres, but by focusing on their tactile and audible trappings, he was able to create sufficiently terrifying images. He believes that, deprived of data available to those with sight, the blind child's mind must work overtime forcing the other senses to create pictures but that there is no doubt that his ability to perceive substance and spirit in the verbal cues of literature is totally adequate and, in any case, subsumed by a larger understanding of the emotional content which informs all literature.

Though by no means indispensable, illustrations play an important role then in the ability, so much a part of reading, to make interior visualizations. Along with other representations, illustrations offer worlds waiting to be explored and could only limit the child's imagination if they were produced mechanically or all in the same style. As we shall see in the chapters which follow, this is certainly not the case with the modern picture-book which has attracted highly gifted artists and authors to share their personal worlds with their readers.

3. *People*

In the long winter evenings, when we had the picture-books out on the floor, and sprawled together over them, with elbows deep in the hearthrug, the first business to be gone through was the process of allotment. All the characters in the pictures had to be assigned and dealt out among us, according to seniority, as far as they would go. When once that had been satisfactorily completed, the story was allowed to proceed; and thereafter, in addition to the excitement of the plot, one always possessed a personal interest in some particular member of the cast, whose successes or rebuffs one took as so much private loss or gain.

Kenneth Grahame, 1898

Stories are about people and the picture-book is probably one of the first places that children meet fictional individuals. Clearly, there are several good reasons why a full description of character and motive is not carried out in the text of a picture-book – the action would be delayed too much, the author would have to resort to difficult abstractions and there would be a very real danger of swamping the child. Adding detail through the illustration and creating character chiefly through illustration is a way round these difficulties and extremely convincing portraits can be given by talented artists. What the child is then able to do is to 'read' the illustration in much the same way as they interpret behaviour in real life. The ability compares with that described by Margaret Donaldson (1978): 'Children are able to learn language precisely because they possess certain other skills – and specifically because they have a relatively well-developed capacity for making sense of certain types of situation involving direct and immediate human interaction.' Just as what people say can, in principle, be understood from what their behaviour intends, so illustration can make the text more comprehensible. According to Nicholas Tucker, (1970) 'children even as young as three years old are sometimes quite successful when asked to infer the likely emotions of certain characters in a visually presented story. But when the same situation is presented to them verbally, without the help of pictures, there is a tendency to focus simply on the outcome of the plot, rather than on anything to do with its characters' possible feelings or motivation.' The important point to make here however is that good illustrations which a child can interpret teach that the nature of the protagonist (or protagonists), their reactions, motives, idiosyncracies, traits, *matter* in a fictional story. To be able to read we must pay attention to the individuality of a character or characters; then we become involved; then we want to know outcomes. I am suggesting that these lessons can be taught through good illustration.

My first example I owe to Maurice Sendak as he describes, in conversation with Jonathan Cott, (1984) Randolph Caldecott's illustrations to *Bye Baby Bunting*. 'The rhyme ends but as you turn the page you see Baby and Mother strolling –

Randolph Caldecott
Bye Baby Bunting

Baby dressed in that idiotic costume with the ears poking out of his head – and up on the hillside a group of about nine rabbits playing. Baby is staring with the most perplexed look at those rabbits, as though with the dawning of knowledge that the lovely, cuddly, warm costume he's wrapped up in has come from those creatures. It's all in that baby's eyes – just two lines, two mere dashes of the pen, but it's done so expertly that they express – astonishment, dismay at life – is this where rabbit skins come from? Does something have to die to dress me?' An illustration of this quality, adding as it does unexpected depths to a simple nursery rhyme, remains steady in the imagination allowing the child to both work on it and to allow it to work back on earlier illustrations to the rhyme.

Another master at winding us in to meet his fictional characters through illustration is Edward Ardizzone, who began his series of picture-books about seafaring Tim with *Little Tim and the Brave Sea Captain* in 1936. Each story in this series provides children with the opportunity to achieve all the impossible heroic tasks they dream about.

Great dangers are faced, great odds are overcome and Tim emerges triumphant and returns home to wonderfully unperturbed parents. The secret of Ardizzone's illustrative art lies not so much in the facial expressions of his characters (though these are expressive enough considering that his style is that of a suggestive sketch rather than a polished portrait) but in his portrayal of legs and arms, particularly perhaps arms. The first half dozen illustrations in the first Tim book tell us much about Tim's nature. We see him first, legs braced, little strong arms hauling up a mast; then we see him seated, cross-legged at the foot of an old boatman, arms inert as he absorbs his lesson in knots; then, with both arms outstretched we see him insisting that his father train his telescope on the ship at sea. From these three openings we are beginning to know this character: active and competent, curious and patient, excitable and single-minded. The text up to this point has simply told us that Tim is obsessed by boats. But there is yet more to Tim. The next three illustrations (all of which, by the way, advance the plot equally as skilfully as they delineate character) show us small Tim seated opposite the elderly captain, balanced politely on the edge of the chair and smiling appreciatively at the Captain. But it is through his arms which are stretched out rather self-consciously to the blazing fire and his legs which are tucked decorously beneath the chair that we understand the mixture of deference and hero-worship that fills Tim's breast as he listens to the Captain's stories. In the next picture, we see an imploring Tim failing to convert his gently patronizing parents to his plan to become a sailor. Arms are again outstretched but this time more openly and with palms uppermost, begging his parents to agree. The text tells us Tim was

Edward Ardizzone
*Little Tim and the
Brave Sea Captain*

sad; the picture tells of his enormous seriousness and determination. The sixth illustration is one of those which Ardizzone himself has commented on. 'One shouldn't tell the reader too much. The best view of a hero, I always feel, is a back view' (in Tucker, 1970). In this back view we see a mournful Tim, bent, gazing down, we presume at his feet, his hands, unemployed, clasped behind his back. Misery and disappointment are summed up in this bowed figure. So our involvement in Tim grows deeper as we are drawn into his dreams and his sorrows. We only know of his adoration of the Captain from the illustration: we only know how hard he fought the battle with his parents from his beseeching stance in that illustration and

whilst the text tells us Tim was 'so sad that he resolved to run away to sea', his enormous grief is 'felt' only through the illustration. It is also important for our empathy that he is drawn alone in this picture, against a lowering sky and an unfriendly sea with an inanimate capstan and bathing hut offering no comfort.

It is at this point that the author starts the story proper with 'Now one day . . .' Enough of Tim's character has been suggested for us to be intrigued and enchanted by this small person and though Ardizzone still conveys an enormous amount through expressive body movement it is from this point chiefly in order to advance the plot and consolidate rather than define Tim's character. Throughout the rest of the story, Tim's seriousness, his perseverance, his resilience, his willingness, his curiosity and his friendliness are known and confirmed again and again through quick strokes of the pen.

It is helpful to use Caldecott and Ardizzone as a sort of touchstone for assessing how other artist/authors create a significant and memorable central character in their books. For children to burst into tears at the end of *The Snowman*

(Raymond Briggs) suggests that they have come to know a distinctive and believable character which is all the more remarkable when you realize that Raymond Briggs dispenses with text altogether here and that his character, being constructed of rather undifferentiated snow, cannot convey fine movements or detail. One of Briggs's most expressive areas is, for instance, the eyebrow (used to such effect in the *Father Christmas* books to reinforce Father Christmas' tendency to grumble) which the snowman is not supplied with. However, through the simple line of the mouth, the movement in the head and again through the use of the arms Briggs allows us to meet this polite, naive, incorrigibly curious, generous and imaginative snowman. Wonder is movingly expressed by a raised arm covering the mouth when faced with the mysteries of electric light, Fairy Liquid and false teeth; concern that they should return home before dawn is indicated by two arms coming up to the mouth and the little coal eyes fastening on the boy's. Simple pleasure is indicated by a broad grin as when he basks in the 'glow' from the refrigerator; his capacity for total ecstasy signified by closed eyes as he luxuriates in the deep freeze. Interestingly, those children who can talk about *The Snowman* in terms of its being a dream or fantasy of the little boy's can also explain that their sorrow at the end is not only at the demise of the wonderful snowman but also at the loss of the dream for the little boy. When asked what sort of little boy he is they will say, "well, he's the sort of boy who's always up to something, always running everywhere, always wanting to play with someone, friendly." If we examine Briggs's drawings of the boy we see the source for these conclusions. The child's woolly hat flies off as he runs eagerly to make his snowman; expressive back views (again) show him looking out of the window almost willing the snowman to come to life as a playmate; a finger raised to his lips alerts us to the forbidden nature of the escapades; a head always turned to the snowman shows us a child eager to learn of another's responses; arms that fly up or encircle the snowman tell us of his protective spirit; open arms that gesture towards a playroom or towards a dining table indicate his generosity; feet that hardly touch the ground as he tears downstairs having been woken by the sun the following morning suggest the extent of his involvement with and concern for his creation. Arms held limply and head bowed mark the final mourning.

Raymond Briggs
The Snowman

Of course children love the adventures these two get up to and Briggs is a master of conveying plot through the comic strip form but the lesson I think *The Snowman* particularly teaches children is again this one of caring about the characters from which curiosity about what will happen to them grows.

Peter, the small boy suffering from sibling rivalry, in *Peter's Chair* (Ezra Jack Keats), is one of the most memorable of this author/illustrator's characters, partly again because of his creator's ability to tell us so much about his feelings through the illustrations. The artist does not allow himself the luxury of

Ezra Jack Keats
Peter's Chair

He picked it up and ran to his room.

fine brush work to convey expression: indeed, it is the *absence* of a mouth line for instance which conveys Peter's misery when he sees his high chair appropriated for his new sister. But in the hunched shoulders and backward glance as he is reproved for making a noise and in the half-concealed peeps he takes at his mother's fussing around his old cradle we learn of the depth of his jealousy. His determination to do something about it is shown in a picture of his brave rescue of his chair when he runs boldly across the page, only Willie, his dog, nervously looking back to check on possible repercussions. A touching picture of Peter kneeling to embrace Willie

who jumps up to lick him reminds us of Peter's emotional needs as he takes the momentous decision to run away. The turning point in the story comes when Peter discovers he has outgrown his chair. A perplexed Peter confirming his fears by physically feeling his sides is watched intensely by his toy crocodile, by Willie and even by the picture of himself as a baby which he has taken for comfort. Recovery of identity and morale is at hand however as he jubilantly pulls off a trick on his mother (arms leap up, fingers outstretched, broad smile crosses his face), earns approval from his father (upturned face, smug smile) and paints his chair for his new sister with devoted concentration shown through an intent look, a kneeling position and a small left hand, fingers spread with a sort of keyed-up excitement.

Anthony Browne is different from the author/illustrators so far discussed in that his style is far more precise, far less impressionistic. Neither Caldecott, Ardizzone, Briggs nor Keats strive for surface exactitude in their illustrations in the way that Browne does. It could be argued that if the faces of characters are indeterminate the child reader will be able more easily to project her own face and persona into them. The imaginative realization of the text may then be facilitated. Hannah, the little girl in Anthony Browne's *Gorilla*, is most exactly drawn. Indeed in every group of children to whom I have read this story recently there has been at least one little girl who 'looks like her'. Despite this photographic exactitude however it is still through stance, arm movement and that all-powerful back view that we learn to 'feel' with Hannah.

Although children get intimations of the bleakness of Hannah's life from the early illustration of Hannah seated opposite her pinched-faced newspaper-reading, black coffee (only) drinking father at breakfast in an ice-blue kitchen, it is at the point where we see Hannah approaching her father in his study that children become involved in her plight and her needs. Hannah stops at a discreet distance from her father's back, standing tensely with a slight deferential bow towards him. Her arms are behind her back in what is a classic submissive gesture and the fingers of one hand nervously pull at her other elbow and sleeve. Feet are neatly together. We do not need to see her face to know what investment she puts in her request that her father take her to the zoo, which is the limit of the information provided by the text. This large picture is

Anthony Browne
Gorilla

followed by a smaller frame where Hannah has dared to move closer to her father but still remains nervously behind him. Dying to distract him but too frightened to make a frontal request she hovers behind his chair, one leg on a rung, her hands on the top of the chair. One child told us she was "sucking the top rail of the chair and jutting it with her teeth". Another said she was kissing the chair because she couldn't kiss her father. From this point on children are imaginatively caught up with Hannah's story and visibly relax as Hannah's dream comes true. No detail is missed as warmth creeps back into her life: the held hand, the piggy-back, the embracing arm, the shoulder ride and particularly the dance where children immediately notice that Hannah is dancing atop the Gorilla's feet. All these details (conveyed only in the illustrations) prepare the reader for the kiss between the Gorilla and Hannah (which might well have been unacceptable without the gentle overtures) and, at last, for contact to be made between father and daughter.

When it comes to the characterization through illustration of animals in children's books, all the above points about stance and expression apply equally. Children are undoubtedly drawn to picture-books which feature animals but the most successful are those books which have this quality of creating a personage whose nature intrigues and whose exploits children care to follow. These creatures' concerns match their own and they feel and relate in ways that children recognize. Again the illustration teaches these understandings. A recent addition to a long tradition of illustrating stories with pictures of animals are the *Ernest and Celestine* books by Gabrielle Vincent which tell of Ernest, a large brown bear, and Celestine, a young mouse. I read the first of these books with

Gabrielle Vincent
Ernest and Celestine

"Wait a minute, Ernest. We're almost ready."

"Oh, Ernest! I'll help you any time!"

a class of four- and five-year-olds and after the reading they pored over four of the illustrations in particular – one of Celestine crying, one of her slamming unwanted soft toys into boxes, one of her shyly peeping round a door and a final one of her being lifted off her feet by Ernest in an ecstatic hug. Older children talk of how the pointing finger, the tugging arm, the covered face, the averted head indicate the rather imperious, 'spoilt' side of this little mouse as she commandeers, reprimands, sulks and weeps; they will then point to the clasping of hands, the jumping in the air, the anticipatory nibbling of fingers which suggest an altogether sunnier but no less passionate Celestine. The patient, sensitive, dependable and earnest Ernest is also known through the illustrations, particularly through the gentle inclining of his head towards his temperamental charge.

Kenneth Grahame &
E H Shepard
The Wind in the Willows

Ernest and Celestine belong to that species of picture-book animals who appear in illustrations dressed in clothes. Again there is a fairly long tradition here, stretching back through Brunhoff, E. H. Shepard and Beatrix Potter to Tenniel though there is an equally strong tradition of animals who, whilst behaving in very human ways, do not sport clothes: Mr. Gumpy's invited guests for instance (in John Burningham's books), Graham Oakley's *Church Mice*, Maurice Sendak's Jenny in *Higglety Pigglety Pop!* and Kathleen Hales' *Orlando the Marmalade Cat* to mention a very few. If 'clothes are the furniture of the mind made visible' (James Laver, in Lurie, A. 1981) then here is a powerful and direct way for illustrators to make their characters distinctive and memorable. It does indeed seem that very few readers forget Peter Rabbit's blue jacket and not only because it is appropriated by the scarecrow. Worn with nothing else and perhaps because blue is a colour traditionally worn by little boys (Tom Kitten also wears blue) it speaks of Peter Rabbit's immaturity and innocence. When Shepard added his illustrations to *The Wind in the Willows* much was communicated through the clothes of the animals. Rat's checked jacket and plus-fours declare his country squire's expansive nature, just as Mole's velvet smoking jacket and Badger's dressing gown speak of more retiring, comfortable personae. Toad, whether in goggles, cap, gaiters and enormous overcoat or in tails, dress shirt, white waistcoat and bow tie and with enormous cigar, displays his wealth conspicuously just as he so generously gives of his extrovert, exuberant if somewhat unsettling personality. And it is waistcoat, checked jacket and pocket watch (and later gloves and fan) which define Tenniel's White Rabbit as the neurotic gentleman he is. All of these telling details come to us through illustration. It may be argued that we are being given stereotypes here; children, however, are coming with fresh eyes to these illustrations and only later learn that their characteristics can be overused.

Children with whom I read the *Ernest and Celestine* books took enormous interest in Celestine's wardrobe. The flimsy pink or blue spotted dresses are loose enough for her to scamper but the delicate frills and flounces suggest that Ernest puts in long hours servicing this ultra-feminine small mouse. Discarded clothes and shoes, scattered around the floor, elicit either delighted recognition or pious censoring from child readers. Ernest seems happiest in long shabby dressing gown and slippers with holes in the toes though he has other outfits, including a splendid Parisian busker's broad black hat and flamboyant yellow scarf ('I feel silly dressed like this' he says), and a velvet-collared jacket for a photograph session. A certain shortage of money is hinted at throughout these *Ernest and Celestine* books, but it remains on the fringe and never stands in the way of Celestine's happiness if the indulgent Ernest can help it. All of these layers of meaning are only accessible through the illustrations, the text consisting simply of snatches of dialogue.

Anthony Browne
Willy the Wimp

The vocabulary of clothes again defines very clearly the character of the gorilla Willy in *Willy the Wimp*. No child is going to be able to see a fair-isle knitted pull-over from now onwards without associating it with the submissive Willy. Significantly, even when he has improved his physique at the body-building club – note how his small yellow (cowardice?) swimming trunks become red (strength, vitality and danger?) – he still wears his fair-isle sweater preparing us perhaps for the denouement where it is clear that his essential courteous nature has not changed. A fair-isle sweater is of course a fairly individual item of clothing and marks the wearer as special; which indeed Willy is compared with the flashy and denim-uniformed gang he has to face. Anthony Browne uses the fair-isle sweater as a leitmotif signalling an unpretentious character in more than this book: Toby in *Through the Magic Mirror*, Hansel in *Hansel and Gretel*, Sean and Katy's father in *The Visitors who came to Stay* all sport this home-spun, cheerful garment and Willy is to be found still sporting his in *Willy the Champ*.

An illustrator who draws attention through clothes to his or her character's personality does so most dramatically when that character is an animal. Obviously the incongruity of an animal in clothing makes us notice and thus the animal's dress adds to our information about the character. It is not that the dress of humans in illustrations is not informative but for some illustrators it is important that the dress of humans be as neutral as possible, perhaps to facilitate empathy. Ardizzone could have quite easily clothed Tim in a sailor-suit (extremely fashionable at the time he was writing) but to do so might have excluded many child readers who see in Tim's indeterminate reddish jersey and grey shorts a symbol for ordinary unprivileged childhood.

There are of course illustrators who want us to notice and interpret the clothes of their human protagonists, amongst whom one could begin with Alice. Tenniel shows us a child dressed in the formal clothes of the Victorian nursery. Her headband, pinafore, puff sleeves and intricate skirt and sash suggest much labour and supervision from nurse. A host of illustrators has subsequently interpreted Alice, all guiding our understanding of this most important fictional child through their individual visions. Arthur Rackham for instance gives us a romantic, Art-Nouveau Alice, far less robust than Tenniel's, who wears a simple, feminine, pink-print dress in which she moves easily and inconspicuously against the background, at one with nature and enjoying a rich inner life. The Russian illustrator Kalinovsky gives us a tall teenage Alice with a wise, penetrating look dressed in a sophisticated check frock, sane amongst surrounding chaos. Ralph Steadman's Alice borrows Tenniel's original clothes but her look is much sharper and more ironic. In a similar way all the various illustrators of fairy tales are able to convey their particular understanding of a character through very differing illustrations of clothing. Cinderella for instance in Errol le Cain's illustrations only has a slightly ragged hem to indicate her poverty. Otherwise her long flaxen hair and dignified stance seem to suggest from the very beginning the elegant future in store. Another illustrator, Bernadette, draws Cinderella as a simple rural child with plait and pinafore, headscarf and apron so that her final transformation to the prince's bride is more appropriately shown against a snow-covered scene riding side saddle with both her and her prince wrapped simply and warmly against the weather. Many lesser illustrators sew innumerable patches on their Cinderella's rags which may convey poverty in the stereotyped way but seldom generate genuine reader interest. The stereotype does convey information however – Ameliaranne's blue gingham apron and wrinkled lisle stockings in Osborne's stories speak clearly of her hard-working and humble background, Madeline's yellow boater with floating black ribbons in Bemelmans' books marks her out as privileged boarding school pupil, but when illustrators can transcend the stereotypical then the character becomes unique as well as recognizable and reader involvement is more reliably ensured.

In this Chapter we have looked at how the illustrator uses facial expression, bodily stance and clothing to convey to the reader information that she or he will use to build a believable and memorable fictional character. If the illustrator can beckon the child into the story in these ways, make the child care about this solemn child or that mischievous creature and show that the investment the child has made will be rewarded by the story-teller's art then it is a lesson that the illustrator can teach in the art of becoming a reader that the writer will continue to teach, building on the illustrator's early work. The child who later can enter the secondary world created only by language may have learnt how to do so from any number of talented illustrators.

4. *Settings*

But it was time to get on for clearly the interest was only just beginning. Over went the next page, and there we were, the whole crowd
of us, assembled in a noble church . . . I turned the page and found
myself free of the dim and splendid church and once more in the
open country.

Kenneth Grahame, 1898

Every author has to introduce his or her reader into the
fictional world of the story. We meet not only the protagonists
but we enter the imaginary space where they live and work,
find adventure and face danger. Just as writers have various
ways of creating settings for their stories, so illustrators, with a
line or a block of colour, may suggest a room or a lonely shore
or, with a mass of detail, fix an exact impression for us enabling
us to enter a particular world rather than an archetypal one.
Sometimes background detail simply marks the environment
in a factual way; sometimes the setting makes its own contribution to the mood of the story; and sometimes the background
is in total conflict with the textual story, thus setting up intriguing ambiguities. Recent narrative theory pays little attention to
the role of setting, perhaps too often taking it for granted or
seeing it as relevant only to classical narrative – and yet none
of us recalls a story without also recalling its location, even if
that is only summoned up by an object or 'prop'. In this
chapter I want to explore how illustrators teach us to extract
from their presentation of background or setting information
that we can use constructively to enter fully into the author's
secondary world. I shall look first at those illustrators who
make least use of background information; then at those
whose settings may be minimal but which are nevertheless
successful at tying the action to a general location; then at
those settings, usually domestic but also occasionally more
exotic, where a mass of realistic detail creates a very specific
scene; then at those settings which convey the countries of the

mind of the protagonist; finally at those settings which sym-
bolize feeling. I shall draw attention to the ways in which
illustrators ensure that we focus on relevant detail or ways in
which an illustrator compels us to 'fill in' the gaps that he or
she deliberately leaves. Young readers who learn how to
absorb the impact of an illustrator's scene setting will be in a
stronger position later to bring meaning to words an author
uses to set the stage.

Dick Bruna
The king

Dick Bruna is an illustrator who virtually cuts out all
background (and all action for that matter) in his attempt to
focus the young reader's attention on the protagonists of his
stories. In his books flat figures, highly stylized and simplified,
stare out at the reader from backgrounds of solid colour.
There are no shadows, there is no light and shade, there are
only primary colours and black outlines. Happiness is always
an upturned mouth; grief – closed eyes, two tear-drops and a

down-turned mouth; and disapproval or anger – a green complexion. Occasionally, as in *The king*, a castle may be represented by a tower made of (we assume) children's building blocks, night time by a crescent on a blue background, but Bruna's intention is not to extend the imagination of his readers, merely to supply an easily identifiable code of emotion. As such he may well be successful (I do remember my children enjoying these books for a short period, though such as still remain are heavily scribbled over), but perhaps by cutting out a context for his characters to act in he creates what in the end remain signs rather than believable characters. You cannot enter these stories because you cannot 'walk round' the characters. Hugh and Maureen Crago (1976) claim that Anna, their daughter, was easily able to deal with subtleties of line and colour, but was initially perplexed by Bruna's 'simplicity'. A diet of Bruna they say 'may produce a child good at dealing

David McKee
Not now, Bernard

"There's a monster in the garden and it's going to eat me," said Bernard.

with stylized figures surrounded by heavy black outlines but unsure of himself outside such a convention'. It is certainly likely that not tying his stories to a specific location makes Bruna highly saleable; his books (which number over thirty titles) have sold twenty million copies across the world. I have my doubts that Bruna plays a major role in the making of literary readers except possibly in the construction the child makes of basic emotions. His stories are usually more rewarding than his illustrations though there is severe reductionism in his re-tellings of traditional tales.

A great favourite amongst children is David McKee's book *Not now, Bernard* (though many an adult is chilled by the theme of pre-occupied parenting that it presents). In this fantasy an ignored child is consumed by a monster who takes his place in the household, the exchange going unnoticed by the child's parents. (The gap in communication between parent

"Not now, Bernard," said his mother.

and child stimulates particularly brilliant picture-books including John Burningham's *Shirley* books and Florence Parry Heide and Edmund Gorey's *Treehorn* books.) David McKee, though we shall see how he can pay a great deal of attention to settings, chooses here a minimal representation of a room and a garden. There is some significant detail – father's bandaged finger, a spreading pool of water under the watered plant – to reflect the reality of the parents' lives, but Bernard moves in a simplified world of vividly coloured interiors and exteriors. Every child can inject into these rather stylized lines and blocks of colour his or her own idea of a house and garden wherein to act out these wild fantasies.

A very different book in a very different style but where an equally sparing use of detail and setting is employed is Sendak and Minarik's *Little Bear*. Here, a whole domestic interior is suggested by putting a broom into an aproned Mother Bear's hand; a judiciously positioned candle right in the centre of a

Else Minarik &
Maurice Sendak
Little Bear

picture with mother and child on either side can stand for the archetypal cosiness and security of bedtime; take the candle away and the same picture only now suffused with blue light tells us Little Bear is ready to sleep. This book is one of a series called *I Can Read* and gives a model of how a 'reader' might be both written and illustrated. The text has lots of dialogue, natural repetition and stories which are all to do with make-believe, motherly love, gentle adventure and quiet mastery and the illustrations never overload the child with extraneous information yet capture the warmth between mother and child and add intriguing detail (Mother's treadle machine and dress-maker's dummy) and symbolic depth (the doves on the roof of Little Bear's home). None of this is easy or desirable to mention in the written text yet it is important for a child to absorb.

Titch, another book for early readers by Pat Hutchins, also makes only minimal reference to a setting in order again, we assume, to focus the reader on the important theme of Titch's

Pat Hutchins
Titch

And Titch had a little tricycle.

relative standing with his older brother and sister. We meet these characters on an empty stage and gradually they enlist the help of props – bikes, kites, musical instruments, tools, garden implements – to help define Titch's diminutive stature. A stylized hill up which to cycle and from which to fly kites is all we see of a setting, but because Hutchins, like Sendak and McKee, is so skilled at directing our eye to the voluble faces of her protagonists, this is all we need to locate the drama of the story. In a sequel, *You'll Soon Grow into Them, Titch*, Pat Hutchins gives the slightly older child a setting which, although still stylized and minimal compared with many illustrators, introduces the child to the fun of discovering how

Pat Hutchins
You'll Soon Grow into Them, Titch

And when Titch needed new socks,

secondary stories can be told through the detail in the background. Thus the mother's pregnancy is echoed in the subplot of the bird and the nest outside; in the growth of bulbs, plants and blossom both inside and out, and in the progress the mother's knitting makes. (She reaches bootees by the time the baby is due.) Seven-year-olds with whom I read this book not only picked up all these stories but also alerted me to the role played by the cat who 'poses for the camera' in every picture, looking out at the reader like a proud compère. The cat's behaviour is tracked enthusiastically through this book, as are all the other stories, but the story of the title is the only story told in the text. This game that children play, where they

they both said,
"You can have our old socks,
they're too small for us."

delight in discovering what the writer is withholding is a feature of Pat Hutchins' earlier and justly lauded picture-book *Rosie's Walk*. It is of course a feature of pantomime and has the effect of ensuring enormous complicity between reader and author/illustrator. It is a technique almost totally unknown to the illustrators of reading schemes, as we shall see in chapter 5. It is, as Margaret Meek (1982) says, 'the beginning of an experience that leads to Jane Austen', and a lesson that the gifted author/illustrator teaches painlessly.

Shirley Hughes, a prolific author/illustrator, draws from life, from gardens and streets around her and from children who could live next door. Some of the impact of her books springs undoubtedly from the closely observed domestic settings of her illustrations. These stories, often for very young children, draw on what is the close-to-hand world of the toddler in this country. *Alfie Gets in First* is typical. We are introduced to Alfie and his mother and baby sister outside a greengrocer's. Mother tucks a cabbage into the pushchair's basket. In the background a purchase is negotiated between customer and shopkeeper. The colour in the picture is concentrated on the family who form a small group in the foreground. The background though not without interest is kept secondary by being painted only in brown. Thus the small reader is helped to save his/her attention for the family whilst not ignoring the fact that we are in a street and out shopping.

Opening two, and whilst not yet into the story proper (but Hughes like many illustrators tells us important things on the title pages), we see small Alfie sprinting away from mother and pushchair. The *absence* of background in this tiny cameo makes us focus on the action and teaches us to switch off now from the activity of shopping.

Opening three, and we are into the story proper. 'One day Alfie and Mum and Annie Rose were coming home from the shops. Alfie ran on ahead because he wanted to get home first.' Everything we have seen we now have echoed in the text – the illustrations have in fact helped us into the text in a very direct way. The illustration shows us a back view of Alfie as he runs off towards the most distinctive house in the Victorian terrace, the one Shirley Hughes draws our eyes to by siting a cat on the gate post.

Opening four shows us a triumphant Alfie sitting on his top step and Mum and Annie Rose arriving a gratifying second. In

Shirley Hughes
Alfie Gets in First

the background we glimpse a lady in blue sweeping her steps on the other side of the street. Shirley Hughes introduces a character but not effusively. We have to read on to know whether she is significant or not. Our eyes also take in a dog and a child in the street.

Opening five and mother has unlocked the door and Alfie marches in straight towards us, the reader. Alfie almost demands that we applaud as he fixes us with a stare. He turns round and we then share his view of Mum as she lifts Annie Rose from the pushchair. Alongside Alfie, in the house, is the all important basket with the front door key on top.

Let Shirley Hughes take up the story from here. 'The hero slams the front door on his Mum and baby sister and then gets stuck inside while a frantic build up ensues on the door-step. I was faced with the design problem of showing both the inside and the outside of the house simultaneously. I hit on the idea of using the actual form of the book, the gutter down the middle where the pages are sewn, as part of the story. So it

became the great divide, and the pictures on each side of the
spread show a double sequence of action in which the non-
reader can be ahead of the text by knowing how Alfie is going
to resolve the problem.' (Hughes, 1985). So the reader has
the chance to watch two stories unfold: one in the street,
where the lady in blue *is* to feature, where the dog has his own
brief moment when he sights the cat who rapidly abandons

"Mmm, looks as though this lock's going to be
difficult to break," said the milkman. But then
Mrs MacNally's Maureen had a very good idea. She
ran to ask the window-cleaner, who was working up
the street, if he would bring his ladder and climb
up to the bathroom window. And, of course, when the
window-cleaner heard about Alfie he came hurrying
along with his ladder as quickly as he could.

her position as sentry, where the milk-man and window-cleaner, whose lives in the street are symbolized by milk-van and ladder, are enlisted to help; and one on the right-hand page where, in the home, Alfie brings about his own solution. Shirley Hughes is particularly concerned to convey the urgent activity in the street; these drawings are crowded and full page. Alfie's isolation however must be stressed and the right-hand pages feature a small Alfie and shopping basket and acres of blank wall and featureless hallway. We know, because we have seen them earlier in his moment of triumphant entry, that friendly and familiar toys lie inside the hall behind the door. But because Shirley Hughes wants her readers to experience Alfie's lonely plight and eventual resourcefulness, we, the reader, stand where the toys are and Alfie's comfortless state is emphasized.

Shirley Hughes is a much appreciated author/illustrator in this country, but it is perhaps appropriate to consider for a moment the criticisms levelled at her that she presents a rather cosy, narrow, white, middle-class environment. Taken to a logical conclusion these criticisms would result in illustrators creating neutral, probably abstract, 'universal' portraits which would be marketable all over the world. The trouble is that information lies in *specificity*: children can learn from illustrators such as Shirley Hughes about another culture in a way that would be impossible if all books were to be produced with an eye to a world market. Obviously if large numbers of minority-group children never see positive images of themselves and their group reflected in the printed or televised images in their society then all the well-documented problems that accompany low self-image become a reality. The answer probably lies in the provision of a rich mixture of culturally diverse picture-books written by author/illustrators who have genuine knowledge of what they are writing about rather than by those who aim to be so neutral that nothing definite is communicated at all. After all we define self-image through exposure to differences as well as similarities. Occasionally an exceptional artist like Leo Lionni in such books such as *Frederick* seems to have universal appeal but we make a big mistake if we start erasing the London buses from books destined for a foreign audience because they are too culture-specific. As Elaine Moss says 'There is no such thing as world culture, culture being something that grows organically from a mixture of specifics: a time, a place, a people, circumstances. The world . . . is still richly various.' (*Signal*, May 1983).

Another artist who creates a very culture-specific setting is Janet Ahlberg in *Peepo!*, written by Allan Ahlberg. The format of their book invites, almost instructs, readers to inspect the scene along with the small baby. The device of the circle cut-out in the page focuses the eye first on the central object in each full-page illustration from where the reader moves out to take in all the family clutter of bedroom, kitchen, garden, living room and the local park as well. Some of the detail is in the rhyming text; most is only in the illustrations and tells the story of soldier-father's visit on home leave to his extended family. This is a period piece for those who remember the nineteen forties where copper dollies, mangles, coal brought in in buckets, wooden clothes horses and stitched celluloid lampshades were part of the scenery, but no reader will fail to find a story to follow through whether it be Grandma's responsibility for the family's linen or father's gradual donning of his uniform. One particularly observant child remarked that women never took their aprons off in those days. Rich detail is evident in other books of the Ahlbergs and makes them books to return to for nothing is included arbitrarily or inappropriately as far as the text is concerned. Hunting the fairy tale characters amongst the scenery is a particular delight of *Each Peach Pear Plum* and identifying the stolen property in *Burglar Bill* is another sleuthing game children play.

In Ahlberg's illustrations carefully chosen and amassed detail extends and elaborates the texts. I want to move now to two books by John Burningham. *Come away from the water, Shirley* and *Time to get out of the bath, Shirley* where text and illustration appear to conflict with each other until the game that John Burningham is playing is understood. Left-hand pages show Shirley's parents (on the beach) or her mother (in the bathroom) and text which gives us the mundane ritual of parental admonishments: 'Mind you don't get any of that filthy tar on your nice new shoes' or 'Look at your clothes all over the floor.' The right-hand pages show us the stories of Shirley's flights of fancy: richly coloured, highly dramatic fantasies of single-handed combat with a bunch of piratical 'tars' and a classic discovery of treasure in the first book; a gallant rescue and further adventures with feudal knights including a watery jousting tournament in the second book. A delicious ambiguity is set up which once resolved draws the reader back for more and more readings. I read these books with several small groups of seven-year-olds and whilst there were always children who found it difficult to know what was going on ("Where are the children her mum tells her to play with? I can't see 'em", "She isn't throwing stones – why does her mum tell her off?"), it was interesting that it was always at the same point that children realized that the right-hand pages show us the landscape of Shirley's mind. The picture where Shirley is being made to walk the plank seems to arouse anxiety amongst children such that in order to handle this disturbing development, they make an 'inferential leap' and they chorus together "It's a dream." "She's imagining it." "It's what she's wishing she was doing rather than sitting with

John Burningham
Come away from the water, Shirley

Don't stroke that dog, Shirley,
you don't know where he's been

her parents on the sand." Slightly older readers guess what Burningham is doing one page earlier as soon as the distant pirate ship is revealed. You have to know that pirate ships are not compatible with a deckchair-and-thermos-flask beach scene – in other words, you have to have been initiated into the 'code' of piracy (*Peter Pan* and *Captain Pugwash* may help here). There are even one or two readers who claim that they knew they were 'inside Shirley's head' as soon as they see her in the rowing boat with the stray dog – "Otherwise the next thing you'd hear would be 'Shirley, get out of that rowing boat at once.'" A measure of the very difficult task that Burningham takes on in teaching his young readers to enter imagined landscapes is the number of children who still ask at the end why she didn't bring any of the treasure she'd

unearthed home. Scathing reminders from knowing classmates produce almost visible adjustment to this difficult but exciting aspect of reading.

Interestingly, the children with whom I read both Shirley books found the second book much easier to interpret: not only had they learnt the counterpointed text and illustration convention from the earlier text but here Burningham helps the reader by 'shrinking' Shirley in order to send her down the plughole. We see a wonderful cross section of her bathroom's plumbing and a tiny Shirley in the waste pipe. I had expected the code of medievalism to be more difficult to enter than that of piracy but Burningham again puts Shirley in a precarious situation (she is suspended over a weir whilst her rubber duck floats on downstream) from which she clearly must be rescued and who better than the knight in shining armour on his white charger whom Burningham paints in the background. There we also have our first glimpse of the King whom Shirley is eventually to topple into the water in the jousting tournament. Children hugely enjoy relating that splash with the *understood* splash that must have occurred in the bathroom. "Now there's water *everywhere*," her mother laments and we see her mopping the floor. Children are learning here not only from what is not written in the text but also from what is not even pictured in the illustration – two telling gaps which Burningham pushes us to fill. One child who particularly enjoyed this juxtaposition went back to the first Shirley book to see if there were similar cross connections there. She decided the best joke was Shirley's mother promising that her father would have a little game with her after his rest (her father is 'seen' fast asleep in his deckchair). Shirley, meanwhile is engaged in the best game of all – digging for buried treasure. It seemed to me that this child through close examination of picture and text was discovering irony. If indeed illustration is helping to develop literary skills of this order then it seems that Burningham is opening up very exciting possibilities for growth in young readers.

From these extraordinary books of Burningham's I want to move to look at several books which I feel contribute to a young reader's understanding of how mood is part of landscape or setting. 'Mood' is an aspect of picture-book experience which translates into words only with difficulty but it is possible to point to how illustrators guide young readers towards this appreciation.

A recent newcomer to the children's picture-book world is Helen Ganly with *Jyoti's Journey*. In pictures which are predominantly collage work (the illustrator acknowledges Sanderson's wallpapers!) the story is told of Jyoti's life in India and of her move to England. No young reader is going to fail to be affected by the contrasting sets of pictures – those of India full of overlaid pattern, bright colour and flowers, those of England full of angular shapes and large blocks of brown, grey and ultimately black – and to pick up the contrasting atmospheres which permeate the book. The writer clearly hopes to convey how dramatically the change to life in this country must affect young children who make the move. Though at first I was saddened by the drab impact England makes (regular rows of terraced houses, high-rise flats) the writer avoids value judgements in the text and leaves Jyoti with some sense of anticipation rather than in overt mourning for her vanished brilliant India. This book is a very direct approach to the child to reconstruct feeling and as such would enable readers to take in this aspect of reading fairly easily.

The author/illustrator who uses colour and pattern, line and wash to convey mood most impressively is Charles Keeping. Children, if not all adults (see Chapter 5), are quite clear about how the illustrations affect them whether in the early brilliantly coloured and patterned books such as *Joseph's Yard* or in the black line and sepia wash illustrations in his more recent books such as *Beowulf, The Highwayman, The Lady of Shalott* and *The Wedding Ghost*. *Sammy Streetsinger* is a model of how colour and design can communicate mood. Sammy, a one-man-band singer, we first meet in a by-pass subway. Warm pinks and browns express Keeping's affection for the city and its inhabitants. Enthusiastic children encircle Sammy, dancing around him to his music. Movement stops abruptly however when a circus ring-master spots Sammy and transfers his act to a circus. The page becomes a rainbow of colours (but they bisect Sammy) until the finale of the act leaves him in a white spotlight of humiliation amidst jeering black and white faces. Sammy's rise to fame is portrayed in ever more psychedelic colour and fragmenting lines but the bright lights of the pop world are set off by chilling views of audiences whose faces appear as skulls in the gloom beyond the stage. Eventually Sammy finds himself back where he

So now he can be found, every day, with his old friends, bringing a little pleasure and gaiety into the lives of the people as they cross under the busy thoroughfare. A truly real entertainer. If you should see him, spare a coin and dance and sing with him.

Charles Keeping
Sammy Streetsinger

started in the underpass and we welcome the return of natural warm colours, a real audience and spontaneous movement. The serious message – the dehumanizing effect of media exploitation – is spelt out in the text but the illustrations explore feeling and mood in ways readily communicated to the reader. Interestingly the text tells the story of Sammy in flashback; this is one literary convention that illustration cannot teach as we process pictures much as we process real life, strictly chronologically.

There are many ways in which a talented illustrator can teach us to respond to created mood. Roberto Innocenti in *Rose Blanche* makes us feel the claustrophobic tension and impending tragedy of his story, set in wartime in Nazi Germany. Colours, here predominantly khaki and dried-blood red, 'sets' that being flat and depth-less bring us unbearably close to the horrors, sudden and dizzying changes of viewpoint rather like varied camera positions all make their contribution and always there is the lone figure of Rose Blanche glimpsed here and there rather like the red-hooded child in the Nicholas Roeg film *Don't Look Now*. The text (by Ian McEwan) tries rather too hard to spell out the messages of the illustrations and ends up by being redundant, but the pictures tell and teach a moving story.

Clearly, *Rose Blanche* is not for the youngest children, but this age group have their tension created in a book such as Ruth Brown's *A Dark Dark Tale*. In this traditional tale we are invited to follow a black cat (a clever device which is guaranteed to make young readers turn the pages) over bleak moor, through low-lying mist in a forest where the eyes of animals watch us, up the steps of a turreted castle, over a cobweb-strewn threshold and past a snarling door-knocker, through a hall of grotesque shadows and so on past watching portraits, billowing curtains, crumbling plaster and leering gargoyles until we are lead to a poor, quivering mouse in its dark, dark box. Children never miss one of these 'spooky' features and rush back to the beginning to frighten themselves anew. It is only to us that these symbols of the eerie are somewhat overworked; for many children they are the first introductions to a language which will be used by many writers they meet subsequently.

All these illustrators give us, through their very differing techniques and impelled by differing intentions, stages on which the actions of their characters will take place. When detail is lacking we have the opportunity to fill in to authenticate a setting; when detail is abundant we can select with discretion, recognize with delight or learn with interest; when impossible contradictions appear we can straddle inner and outer worlds almost simultaneously; when colour and line express the illustrator's strong feeling we can pick up the mood and deepen our understanding.

5. Story

Well, no doubt they were now being married. He and She, just as always happened. And then, of course, they were going to live happily ever after; and *that* was the part I wanted to get to. Storybooks were so stupid, always stopping at the point where they became really nice; but this picture-story was only in its first chapters, and at last I was to have a chance of knowing *how* people lived happily ever after. We would all go home together. He and She and the angels and I; and the armour-man would be invited to come and stay. And then the story would really begin, at the point where those other ones always left off.

Kenneth Grahame, 1898

A child's very first picture-books are often single-concept 'naming' books in which the child is encouraged to label discrete items or single actions. Valuable though this activity is, especially because of the turn-taking talk which accompanies it, there is a world of difference between this and the interpretation of a series of pictures in sequence which depends upon the ability to see relationships between objects and to draw inferences. Shirley Hughes (1985) speaks of 'that wonderful moment when a baby gets hold of a book and suddenly realizes that the image on one page connects with the one overleaf,' and Marilyn Cochran-Smith (1984) equates the teaching of reading with the teaching of inference (though I regret her emphasis on the teaching rather than the learning).

It was Shirley Hughes's wordless picture book *Up and Up* that convinced me that children learn essential narrative structures, story shape and story schemata from pictures. Because this book has received such acclaim for its excellent draughtsmanship and the inventiveness of the visual techniques, there has been less attention given to the literary literacy that it both demands and teaches. But as Shirley Hughes (1985) herself says, 'Not even the most dazzling display of design and colour technique can make up for a weak story-line.' Beyond all the visual devices that she employs there is a strong and complex story and the pictures teach children one thing about stories – they keep going. Of course, we have to be 'visually literate' to interpret the signs which tell the story; but we fail, if we fail, to understand this story not because we don't notice small detail and effects of composition, but because we don't know enough about reading, about how stories work. Gordon Wells (1985) speaks of readers needing to 'follow and construct a narrative and expository sequences, recognize causes, anticipate consequences and consider the motives and emotions that are inextricably bound up with all human actions and endeavours'. All this, it seems to me, is what the reader of *Up and Up* is engaged in. It is very clear that if a reader of this book is not prepared to supply what the author omits, then no amount of skill in identifying Shirley Hughes's graphic brilliance will bring about understanding. I have now read this book with a very wide range of readers and it would appear that it is familiarity with literary conventions or a willingness to learn them that enables readers to notice the visual detail, to seek out confirmation of their expectations in the pictures. If you are an inexperienced reader, you do not know what to look for in the pictures.

The story is about a small but determined 'little female Icarus' who wants to fly. She eventually succeeds, much to the consternation of family and neighbourhood, enjoys her aerial escapades and eventually comes down to earth and returns to her breakfast.

Now part of the act of reading is knowing that the early stages of a story require a high level of toleration of uncertainty on the part of the reader; or, to use Iser's words, we are 'confronted by narrative techniques that establish links between things we find difficult to connect so that we are forced to reconsider data we at first held to be perfectly straightforward.' Shirley Hughes's need at the beginning of *Up and Up* is to inform us that her small girl has a burning ambition to fly. She does this through analogy – the end papers give us an aerial view of the girl's neighbourhood with very prominent birds flying around. We then see the girl imitating a bird by flapping her arms, then making paper wings, then rising aloft through balloon power. Eventually she receives a chocolate egg which she crawls into and eats her way out of to discover that she now has ingested magic powers. There are some readers influenced by the large black birds of the end paper, the bird on the dedication sheet and the birds in the first frames who cannot move from an early conviction that she wants to *be* a bird to the more important generalization that she is interested in the ability to fly which birds happen to have. These readers then have great difficulty interpreting the pictures of the magic egg taking effect – and indeed say that she is about to be sick! Others will say that so excited is she by the arrival of the egg that she has given up wanting to be a bird and only the more confident will revise this opinion when they read on and find she has indeed achieved her ambition. The point is that readers learn to be flexible, to put what appears to be critical information into a subsidiary position in the interests of forming a generalizable basis on which to erect the developing story. Interestingly, although more than half of the readers had difficulties in establishing this opening basis, if they did not resolve it by frequent scanning back and forth, it was always resolved on a second reading. One reader who had agonized over whether the birds were thrushes, starlings or blackbirds on the first reading, returned to state simply, "She's obviously hooked on this idea of flying" and rescanned the end paper with very different expectations, no longer seeing the large birds as so significant but instead spotting the small girl in her garden and the step-ladder from which she practised flying. Shirley Hughes has taught us how to see. This confirms Iser's statement – 'It is a common enough experience for a person to say that on a second reading he noticed things he had missed when he had read the book for a first time, but this is scarcely surprising in view of the fact that the second time he is viewing the text from a different perspective' (1974).

The next problem for readers depends for its solution on even greater familiarity with story schemata. Our small protagonist has been aiming to reach a goal – in her case flight – and it appears she has achieved it. But clearly, a quick flick through the remaining pages tells us there is more to be unfolded. The heroine needs to encounter further obstructions so that she may resolve them and to some extent this is both what happens and what many readers expect. But the most responsive readers know that half the fun of any daydream is the position one gives oneself as all powerful at the centre of onlookers who are basically passive. So the real aim of our heroine is not just flight, but an opportunity to amaze and impress everyone. Shirley Hughes gives lots of clues of course – our heroine assesses her father's reactions out of the corner of her eye, she does not just fly, she is an enormous exhibitionist, somersaulting and pirouetting after her swagger across the ceiling (indeed one reader called her "young madam" from about this point onwards), but only if you can

Shirley Hughes
Up and Up

bring a personal understanding of the inner world of fantasy to these pictures can you begin to interpret what is happening. All the illustrated reactions to our young heroine's adventure are how the girl, in her imagination, wants them to react. So her parents are paralysed with shock and then filled with consternation – not as some readers believe angry at having

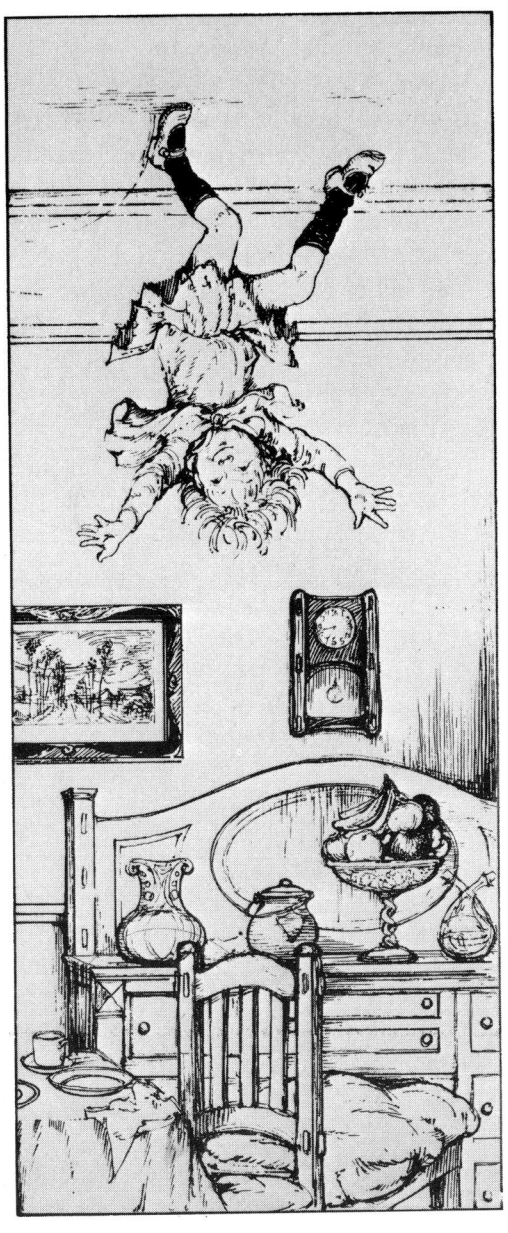

their breakfast and newspaper-reading interrupted, and keen to let her continue her acrobatics outside. We see them at an open door, but surely they have not opened it. The bus queue cannot take their eyes off her, not as some would have it because they are eager to have revenge on her for knocking their hats off (though there is a clear example of affronted dignity in the business man), but because she is so extraordinary a sight. Similarly the stall-holder, though initially angered by the overturned basket, is much keener to follow this phenomenon than to reprimand her. The role of the scientist (or ''mad professor'' as he is invariably called) is particularly difficult to construe unless you are able to understand that the heroine's new aim is a demonstration of control. The professor's grim determination not to be outwitted is no match for her inventiveness: even when he catches her from his hot air balloon she wriggles free of her cardigan and uses the fractured television aerial of earlier cavortings to puncture his balloon and so engineer her own descent. The most difficult picture in the whole book to interpret, if you have not put this small girl in the centre of her own fantasy, is one near the end showing a handshake between the professor and the girl. Some readers interpret this as the girl's thanking the professor for rescuing her, some as her consoling him for his unsuccessful pursuit; yet others see the handshake as his forgiving her for leading him a song and dance. But after a triumphant flight such as hers the only appropriate response is congratulation which the professor deferentially offers and which she magnanimously receives. It is no reflection on Shirley Hughes's

artistic ability that this frame is so frequently misconstrued by readers; but it is a reflection on the complexity of the story and the level of familiarity readers have with the conventions underlying it. Second readings clarify this picture to such an extent that readers hardly believe that they could have so misinterpreted it on the first reading. (If you feel I am too partisan to my own reading here I will call on Paul Goodman (1954) to defend me. 'In the beginning (of a narrative) anything is possible; in the middle things become probable; in the ending everything is necessary.' The working out of a plot is as Seymour Chatman (1978) indicates a 'process of declining or narrowing possibility'.)

Much as I would like to linger a moment on Shirley Hughes's graphic brilliance (I like particularly the way both birds and the girl are forever 'escaping' from the frame), a wordless book like *Up and Up* is only one way of telling a visual narrative. It is a way which owes a great deal to the cinema (or vice versa) in that as far as possible the strip form allows the reader to follow movement and progression with the minimum need for 'guessing' or 'filling in the blanks' between one picture and another. Of course there is always some imaginative leaping to be done but it is kept to a minimum and I suspect this is one of the reasons for the enormous popularity of strip cartoonists, whether Raymond Briggs, Hergé, or the anonymous authors of comics.

As soon as the illustration of a written story is the issue, an illustrator is faced with different problems. Brian Wildsmith claims 'There are roughly, at a quick count, two ways of illustrating a book. The first is to give, shall we say, a diagrammatic representation of the text; the sole aim is putting the text into picture form. The other way is to enlarge on the text, to create a pictorial form that is at one with the text and yet is a thing unto itself' (in Samuels, 1970). Maurice Sendak describes his aim as an illustrator 'I wanted at all costs to avoid the serious pitfall of illustrating with pictures what the author has already illustrated with words' (in Egoff *et al*, 1969). Ardizzone (also in Egoff) also feels strongly that illustrations must elaborate a text which should give no more than the bare bones. Ardizzone then goes on to make a case for picture books to be a one-man product, text and illustrations coming from the pen of one creative mind.

Ardizzone would have to concede that there are many successful picture-books produced by teams – one has only to think of *The Story of Ping, The Elephant and the Bad Baby, Mr. Rabbit and the Lovely Present, Angry Arthur, Burglar Bill, John Brown, Rose and the Midnight Cat, The Shrinking of Treehorn, Meal One*, the *Captain Najork* books not to mention the work of illustrators like Keeping, Le Cain and Anthony Browne who can give old stories new perspectives. However, there are many, many picture-books which fall into the trap to which Ardizzone, Sendak and Wildsmith alert us – that of sticking to the text in so literal, tight and obvious a way that the reader has no space either to interpret the text with relative freedom (which might sometimes be possible if the text were left unillustrated), or interpret the illustrations in such a way that they illuminate the text.

The prime example of course of this sort of illustrated story which I feel contributes nothing to a child's understanding of narrative conventions is the reading scheme. I can find no understanding by the compilers of reading schemes of the role that illustrations might play in developing reading competence. One looks in vain for the invitation to jump from what is left unsaid in the text to what is deliciously described in the pictures (as in *Rosie's Walk*). One looks in vain for the encouragement of complicity between reader and hero (as in *Not now, Bernard*). One never finds a deadpan text, offset by hilarious pictures, which keeps one searching for connections and cohesions (as in *I Hate My Teddy Bear*). The detective work encouraged by gifted illustrators in books for even the youngest child is totally absent from the reading scheme. If you notice that Celestine has dropped Gideon before Celestine herself realizes and before the narrator tells you, what an involvement in the story the author ensures. If you can pick up from the pictures the sickening envy that Madeline's eleven

Ludwig Bemelmans
Madeline

companions feel after observing the hospitalized Madeline's privileges (including the appendix scar), then you know, in advance of Miss Clavel, what is troubling these eleven small girls in the middle of the night. What satisfaction that gives! If through brilliant composition skills and the device of a mysterious and compelling cat, you are led into a book so that each page seems to ask 'Will you go through this door?' and you have to answer yes and turn the page (as in Ruth Brown's *A Dark Dark Tale*) or if, through the clever use of half pages, you are drawn through a house to the very bed of a reader like yourself (as in Ron Maris' *My book*), then you know something about entering a secondary world that reading schemes cannot begin to teach.

There are explanations though no excuses for the limitations of the illustrations in reading schemes. Research project after research project (summarized by Samuels, 1970) has 'proved' that pictures interfere with reading because they distract the reader's eye away from the print, even enabling the reader to guess without looking at the print. There is never any recognition of the more holistic view of reading that suggests that readers need to bring knowledge from personal experience and other texts to the reading process, that context and preceding text enable us to form predictions, that text is sampled to confirm expectations. Word identification is their model for the reading process so it is with a complete absence of irony that they conclude that pictures can build background information, prompt when a new word is not recognized, introduce the unknown, influence attitudes, motivate the child, carry the theme of the story, hold the child's attention – but not help with reading. With this sort of research finding it is no surprise that producers of reading schemes avoided anything approaching an interesting or extending or interpretive illustration. And if illustration was really rather a bad thing, then it was prudent not to acknowledge the illustrator in the credits.

I had wondered whether any of the newer reading schemes which, after all, boast 'real stories' and 'artful illustrations' would succeed in creating the combination of graphic art and narrative in which the sense of the story is completed and extended by the illustrations. One sets about the search however with no great optimism: nowhere in the five schemes I checked through – Story Chest (E. J. Arnold), Oxford Reading Tree, Open Door (Nelson), Puddle Lane (Ladybird) and Ginn 360 was an illustrator writing his/her own text. As we have seen, this is not essential for a satisfying and enriching experience, but if an illustrator chooses to illustrate someone else's text then that text needs to be special enough to provoke a creative response. One or two artists in the Story Chest series who have been offered traditional tales to illustrate seem to me to have produced illustrations which leave the reader some work to do in terms of prediction and inference. Christine Ross, stimulated by the same story which Ruth Brown illustrated, produces *In a dark, dark wood*, which invites us to predict in each picture where next the unseen host will take us. In *Plop!* she lets the reader see the heron stalking the frog before either narrator or frog is aware. The question then asked by the text ('Can he see the big bird?') is only fully answered in the illustration where we see the small frog evade the heron just in time. In a text of thirteen words it is no mean achievement to induct readers into the hermaneutic code; it is of course only made possible through the illustrations which extend the bald text. (One has to say that this book pales into insignificance beside Pat Hutchins' *Rosie's Walk* but it is quite a find amongst standard reading schemes.) Story Chest also has, in Martin Bailey who illustrates *The big toe*, another traditional tale, an illustrator who plays with perspective and page layout in ways quite unique in reading schemes. Using

Martin Bailey
The big toe

camera techniques which make foregrounded objects loom impossibly large he transfixes readers with the image of the vast hairy toe which is 'found' in fact on the title page before the text begins. The old woman does not merely find this toe; she examines it with a magnifying glass. Going home is no conventional affair; we sit in the old woman's bicycle basket along with her shopping and the grotesque toe. Finally she returns it to its owner with a disdain conveyed by outstretched arm and splayed fingers. Of course, none of this is in the text; the reader is invited to create a character of this old woman and to dwell on the physical reality of the object she finds.

Amongst a great deal of indifferent drawing and banal vision, these two artists stood out but Puddle Lane and Oxford Reading Tree produced no surprises, illustrators appearing to pay no attention to the needs of the reader to be surprised, to discover, to absorb atmosphere, to detect secondary stories, to confirm or modify early surmises. Ginn 360 have, amongst their Magic Circle 'extension' books, two illustrated stories by Tomie de Paolo which are exceptional but in their reading programme, not even Mercer Mayer can make other than duplicated comment in his illustrations for *Kim Ann and the Yellow Machine*. Never is he allowed to employ his skill in allowing the pictures to run ahead of the text and push the action forward, though he cannot help but create unusually individual characters.

My hopes were raised when I saw the names of Tony Ross and David McKee amongst the illustrators for Nelson's Open Door books. Sadly, however, the repetitive, monotonous text of *New Boots for the Dragon* (stage 3:8), so clearly predicated on the assumption that children need to be taught words through reinforcement, has not enabled David McKee to do more than create some mildly interesting individuals who exchange expressive glances but who remain tied to the shoe shop and carry out the limited transaction of purchasing boots, which is the sole content of the written text. I cannot imagine that David McKee enjoyed producing twenty-nine separate frames where the only changes that are rung are in the colours and sizes of boots offered to the small dragon. Given the freedom to choose his own text who knows what surreal scenario this creator of *I Hate My Teddy Bear* might have produced. But Tony Ross's illustrations for *Elephants going to bed* (Blue Fun Book 3) are a demonstration of how much a talented illustrator can extend and yet not submerge a very simple text. In a series of pen and wash sequential pictures which use best cartoonist techniques to convey movement, Tony Ross adds incident, character, mood and detail to a text which, in only twelve words, tells of how three elephants go up to bed, have a bath, jump on the bed and fall asleep. Tony Ross, like so many illustrators, starts his story on the title page, where a dressing-gowned elephant skids on a bar of soap and sends his teddy bear flying. Teddy bear (now outside frame) is retrieved on the way up to bed but the soap is of no interest to bathing elephants and remains outside frame. Other details – various entwinings of trunks and tails and hot water bottles – convey the mood of the story. Mother arrives on the scene (again she emerges from behind the frame), unmentioned in the text, and puts the jumping trio to sleep but not before a picture (can it be father elephant's portrait?) is knocked off the wall. The small teddy bear ends as it began, a neglected victim of youthful elephantine exuberance; only his thin legs extend from behind the frame. I suspect that Tony Ross took over control of this production – the words 'Go to bed' are made to issue from mother elephant, almost in best Ardizzone bubble fashion, and even on the series' standard cover that limp teddy bear is allowed to break the frame.

It seems then to be more accidental than intentional if reading scheme publishers find illustrators who are able to do more than simply duplicate or parallel what is said in the text. There is actually no such thing as simply doubling up on information; because the medium of illustration is different from that of words, it forces the illustrator to supply detail that is taken for granted in the text. But it is when an illustrator can extend a text in ways that cannot be taken for granted, in ways which challenge our pre-conceptions, that a picture-book can offer an intense experience for the reader. The only reason why more reading scheme stories cannot be like *Elephants going to bed* is the limited view that publishers and their advisers and customers have of what role illustrations could play. Clearly on one level Tony Ross's illustrations are distracting; but their diversionary nature must surely not only attract children to the book again and again (no small achievement in a reading scheme) but also notify children that narrative is advanced not only through major events but also through minor supplementary events. Learning to place actions in sequence is essential behaviour for a reader; illustration can teach this first lesson in plot-shaping when both publisher and illustrator perceive its potential.

The reading scheme world only occasionally then invests in illustrations' potential to teach narrative. We have yet to see a wordless picture-book along the lines of *Up and Up* or *The Snowman* in a reading scheme and Tony Ross's book is a very special discovery in a world where the careless, superfluous, over-literal illustration dominates. In the trade world however there are several word-less picture-books now which cover a wide range of narrative difficulty and some are surprisingly difficult. *Changes, Changes* by Pat Hutchins 'for the very youngest' poses some difficulties because of the stylization – one five-year-old thought the flames were chicken feathers – and more generally because the characters keep dismantling the settings in which they have to operate. *Sunshine* by Jan Ormerod keeps within the known world of the small child and takes its narrative sequence very carefully, yet even here a four-year-old thought the dark smoke of burning toast was night falling at first. Time to look carefully is critical here. *The Great Flood* by Peter Spier makes big narrative leaps and Charles Keeping's two wordless books *River* and *Inter-City* will only be understood by readers willing to do 'quite half the labour' and able to supply 'deleted' material. Mitsumasa Anno's books, including *Anno's Journey*, of enormous interest to patient, well-travelled, 'cultured' adults, neverthe-less enable the sharp-eyed child to identify the main pro-

Jan Ormerod
Sunshine

tagonist as he wanders through panoramas of life amongst numerous mini-dramas which crop up and die away as the pages are turned. In the area of minimal text with extending pictures, we have not only the perfect *Rosie's Walk* but also some quite brilliant stories published by Oxford including Brian Wildsmith's *Cat on the Mat*, a demonstration if ever there was one of what can be done with the classic reading scheme text. Only in the pictures (wonderfully perspective-less, teaching children about art as well as literature) do we read the story of how a proprietory cat resents her particularly large and beautiful mat filling up with ever larger intruders whom she finally and dramatically expels. She resumes sole ownership and the text repeats the opening line 'The cat sat on the mat.' The text on its own has no power to raise expectations; but even on the first opening we wonder why the mat has to be so large, and by the second opening and the arrival of the dog we already have interaction and potential drama. *Gregory's Dog* by William Stobbs (also Oxford) would surely upset the reading scheme purists: Gregory is training his dog and everything in the text is flatly contradicted in the

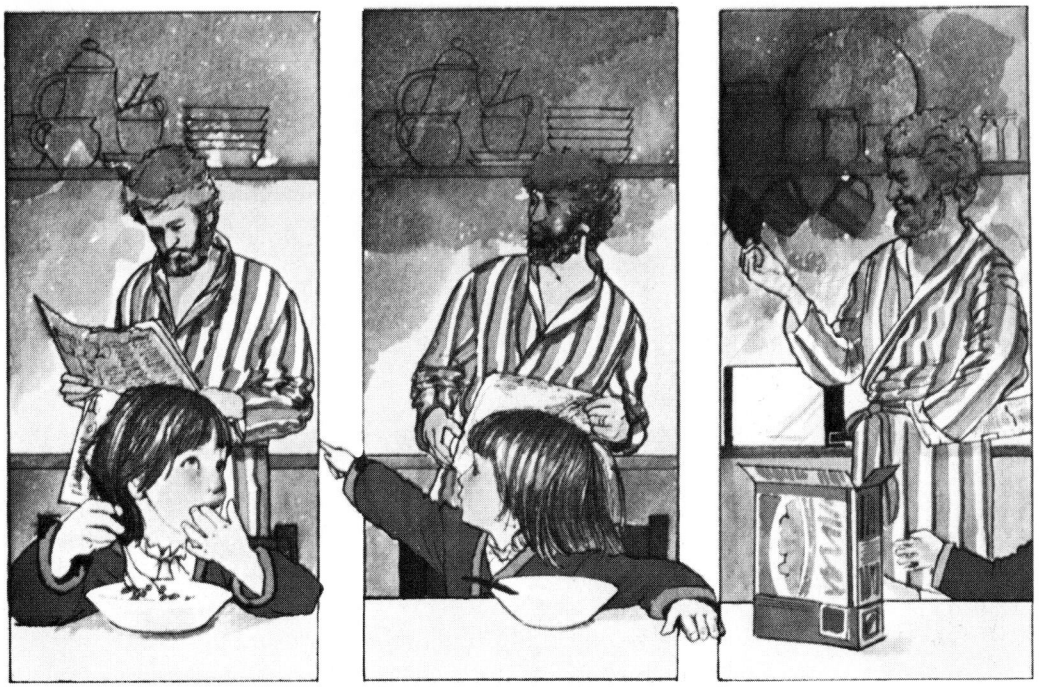

illustrations thus echoing life where doubtless instructions to dogs to "sit" frequently result in a standing up on the hind legs. Only at the end do text and illustration tell the same story. 'Gregory says "Eat." ' And the dog eats.

I have tried in this chapter to isolate the particular contribution that illustrators can make to the developing narrative understanding of readers. By focusing on the books with minimal or no text the bones of narrative are more apparent; as texts become longer, illustrations may be used less to tell continuous story and more to guide readers' grasp of significant points in the plot (as well as create character and setting and mood as earlier discussed). However, there are several longer texts where illustrations still do very much more than fill in by 'verisimilitude' and some of these will be discussed in the next chapter, and many of them have been touched on already in preceding chapters. I will close this chapter by looking at Anthony Browne's *Piggybook*. It shares with his other books an extraordinary belief that the text and the illustrations can take it in turns to tell the story. Where other illustrators would need to ensure that readers had not missed the fact that the chauvinist male members of the Piggott family were turning into pigs, Browne makes no verbal mention of this radical development except to gradually insert a different quality of verb so that where once boys shouted and mumbled they now squeal and grunt in what has become their pigsty, literally as we see in the pictures, metaphorically as we understand in the text. This is not the place to identify the slow progress to piggery that Browne, in characteristic surrealist way, documents in his pictures, but in the avid search for embryonic snouts in unlikely places that children undertake, they learn a great deal about narrative as well as about male chauvinism. No climax is more dramatically handled than when the absent mother returns and her shadow falls from the doorway onto a floor where husband and sons are 'rooting' for 'scraps' – "Please come back", they snuffle. The next illustration shows them utterly transformed into pigs, on their knees at her feet. Clearly from such a position there is no going back and – if the story is to be believed – all learn their lesson and live henceforth a healthy life of mutual co-operation.

In a book of this quality the reader moves constantly between the text and the pictures in a complex process of picturing text and verbalizing pictures, allowing one to complement the other in a way that will lay a foundation for the complex transformation of text into experience that will come with reading solely verbal text. Whilst there are visual conventions that have to be learnt and whilst pictures are culturally specific and therefore not unproblematic, the fact that pictures can be understood from a relatively early age enables the illustrator who enjoys the challenge to display a range of story-events with or without text which adds to the reader's growing command and understanding of narrative.

Anthony Browne
Piggybook

6. *Themes*

Fluent readers and absolute beginners both need picture books as the beginning of thinking.

Margaret Meek, 1982

All art creates for the audience an imaginary world which, because it is more ordered, is at once more dynamic, more complex, more surprising than reality. It shows us life more broadly and more deeply than we normally encounter it, and it mirrors back to us aspects of ourselves that we may or may not consciously recognize. In this chapter I want to look at those author/illustrators who through the medium of the picture-book communicate to the child some of the messages that all great art can convey — messages which reflect our humanity, our individual and collective existence. The forms, 'symbolic of human feeling' (Susanne Langer, 1953), that the child meets in the picture-book will not be the only aesthetic forms that the child meets but they are amongst the earliest created specifically for the child. Because of their special accessibility, they give the child an early encounter with what literature on its own will effect later.

In the earlier chapters some of the ways in which illustrators offer the child entry to literary conventions and layers of emotional and cognitive understanding have been isolated and discussed. I shall now turn to a handful of books where the illustrator/authors have been at pains to integrate text and picture to produce for the reader a unified and shaped aesthetic experience. If I have tended in the bulk of this investigation to promote the artwork at the expense of the text, it is to correct an adult tendency which considers literary merit alone. The textual content of the books I am going to discuss can be simple or quite demanding, exploring the full range of humanity's concerns both contemporary and local, ageless and universal but it is the artwork which fills in, extends and enhances the written text so that the child is enabled to make emotional and intellectual forays into the complex meanings that the authors want us to share and create. There is an answer in these books to the criticism occasionally voiced that the children's book world presents too cosy and reassuring a view of childhood; that children's books do not face up to the challenges that children face. Growing up, meeting change, separating from parents, developing a sense of being one's own person, developing an awareness of social expectations and responsibilities are themes present in many of the books already discussed in earlier chapters but are evident particularly in the books I choose to discuss finally.

It was probably Maurice Sendak's *Where the Wild Things Are* (published in 1963 in America) which most dramatically challenged the conception of a secure childhood and an unchanging social order. Dismay (on adults' part) that those monsters would disturb children brought a philosophical defence from Sendak in his 1964 Caldecott Award acceptance speech: 'From their earliest years children live on familiar terms with disrupting emotions, fear and anxiety are an intrinsic part of their everyday lives, they continually cope with frustration as best as they can. It is through fantasy that children achieve catharsis. It is the best means they have for taming Wild Things' (in Lanes, 1984). But it was not only the content of the book that made it a remarkable event in the picture-book world; the controlled handling of the illustration was also enormously exciting. The child was helped to move from the constraining world of reality into fantasy by Sendak's literally expanding the frame, dissolving Max's bedroom walls into a forest before our eyes. The return is similarly symbolized by the frame contracting as Max returns to the reality of a dinner still hot, emblem of the unseen mother who still loves him despite his tantrum. Those three double pages of wild rumpus where the text dared to let the pictures do the telling made adults and children alike reconstrue the role of illustration.

Outside Over There, published in 1981 after five years' toil, has provoked comparable if not more controversy. In every way this text offers the greatest potential for readers to contribute actively to the making of meaning. Everybody with whom I have read this book becomes a co-author in Iser's sense. A group of eight-year-olds worked seriously on trying to build up a satisfying reading but ultimately turned it aside because there were too many unanswered practical problems – they allowed the goblins to be invisible to Ida but how could the ladder be also? They allowed Ida to fly, but how did she know in advance that the yellow cloak was magic? How did the goblins know Ida's name? ("Terrible Ida," the goblins said, "we're dancing sick and must to bed.") And, most importantly, how did those goblins/babies feed themselves? Some said it was a scary book – "I'll be scared when I next look after my baby sister" – and one said that it was only suitable for babies because they'd not know what kidnapping was! Despite their impatience with aspects of it, one girl suggested that because Ida looked bigger and older at the end she must have learned something – perhaps not to leave babies under open windows. Two twelve-year-olds (boys) were able to add that they felt the father was testing the daughter but they were still concerned with practicalities – where did the goblins keep the ice baby? Under their cloaks? If so, why didn't it melt? Two seventeen-year-old girls took great pains to piece together the symbolic meanings. They believed that in the full moon, the caves, the eggshells and the encroaching sunflowers they had found images which explained 'honeymoon' and 'bride' and 'wedding' in the text, but they resented what they believed to be Sendak's message that young girls should don the mantle of female responsibility and what they felt was his equating of sexuality with motherhood. Colleagues (along with many of those who have written about this book – see Aidan Chambers, 1983, 1985; Jane Doonan, 1986; de Luca, 1984; M. Steig, 1985; B. Keifer, 1985) are clearly impressed by the power the book has to lodge in the memory, where its images – for instance the ship wrecked in the storm which rages outside Ida's window – can be worked on long after the book is laid down. Everyone has been fascinated to learn from Sendak of some of the sources which inspired the book. These include the much publicised kidnapping of the Lindbergh child, a childhood book with a girl in a yellow coat, memories of being looked after by his sister, work on illustrations for Grimm's *The Juniper Tree*, German fairy tales generally and painters, particularly Philip Otto Runge whose painting 'The Hulsenbeck Children' contains the motifs of the sunflowers, white picket fence and solemn babies that echo in *Outside Over There*, and above all perhaps Mozart and The

Magic Flute, to whom Sendak has paid direct and indirect tribute throughout the book. These influences explain why the book looks like it does; the wide range of responses that the book encourages suggests that readers make meanings for themselves as they follow Ida's painful journey into self-understanding. Or maybe they follow the baby's adventures. Sendak claims that this book is 'about early childhood and the problem of the inexplicable arbitrariness of life to a child'. (Television programme, 1986). No other picture-book makes the reader more aware of the act of reading; no other picture-book I have come across benefits more from a collaborative reader-response approach in which individual experiences

Maurice Sendak
Outside Over There

The ice thing only dripped and stared,
and Ida mad knew goblins had been there.

are exchanged and individual frustrations supported. It is not a book which gives away its secrets easily.

Charles Keeping is another author/illustrator whose work has been problematic for teachers and librarians though, like Sendak, he has received several awards. Aidan Chambers (1985) tells of a librarian convinced that Keeping's books never leave the shelves because his illustrations are 'too sophisticated', and many teachers feel that his books are too sombre and depressing in theme, too puzzling and abstract in illustration, too obscure in overall intention. These criticisms may well have had an effect on Keeping as in the eighties he wrote fewer of his own texts and reverted to the pen, pencil and soft chalk drawings of his early seventies books. Only *Sammy Streetsinger* (see Chapter 3), published in 1984, employs his own text and distinctive use of colour.

This may be an appropriate moment to consider the subject of 'abstract' illustrations in children's books. Clearly of all the illustrators we have considered, Keeping is most obviously influenced by the 'modern' art movements of this century. Even to the untutored eye, the blocks of transparent colour, shafts of light, geometric shapes, use of vigorous super-imposed line, strong patterning and sculptured figure shapes remind one of painters such as Sutherland, Piper and Henry Moore. That a serious illustrator of children's books should be influenced by the art of his times is not surprising, but it seems to make those in charge of children anxious. The feeling that children will neither like nor understand such illustration is strengthened by knowledge that, when questioned, children claim to prefer realistic illustration and aim for realism in their own drawings and paintings. This is generally endorsed by psychologists such as Howard Gardner (1982), 'No longer intent upon following their own artistic promptings, children at this age (7–12) become intent on drawing objects and scenes accurately. They strive for realism, in terms of either photographic resemblances or of conventions embraced by their culture: they prefer realistic works by others and often scorn those that deviate significantly from representationality.' Numerous studies claim to show children's preference for realism in artwork (G. Smerdon, 1976). Many of these resear-chers go to great lengths to reduce the variables in their experiments. They exclude colour, they keep the content the same but vary the degree of abstraction, they exclude pictures of animals and people, they keep the pictures the same size, they control the quality of draughtsmanship. However, what they totally fail to do is to realize that children's responses to illustration are a part, an inseparable part, of their total response to a text. Illustrations cannot be treated like isolated paintings; they are integrated and work in harmony with the written text in such a way that the whole is always greater than the parts. It is unfortunate if this fact is ignored and if adult suspicion of Keeping is fed by these misleading findings.

It certainly seemed to me that adults' misgivings were misplaced when I read Keeping's *Through the Window* with seven-year-olds. Far from finding the illustrations 'contentless' (an accusation levelled at abstract pictures) they found much to comment on; far from finding them too difficult (as was predicted for these 'pre-operational' children) they explained

Charles Keeping
Through the Window

much of their resonances to me; and far from being scornful of their deviation from simple representation, they were actively interested in the techniques Keeping employs and fascinated to learn, for instance, that these illustrations were originally painted on layers of perspex. It was indeed through examining some of the strangeness of his illustrations that they were able to absorb some of the power and beauty of this story. Almost the first detail that they picked on was the church cross. They originally interpreted this on the title page as an indication that we were in a graveyard but by the second opening they realized it was part of a reflected skyline and by the third they had established that it was on a church and that we had had three glimpses of it (through curtains, reflected onto glass, a shadow on the pavement) before we saw it fully through the window. We see this cross twice more; once when 'Old Soap' the old woman is introduced, once when we meet her dog. By working on this detail (which I had certainly failed to notice) they established a mood for the whole story and were able to use its symbolic force to explain the final death of Old Soap's dog and its 'resurrection' in Jacob's drawing on the window. Similarly, they noted immediately that the lace curtains through which Jacob gazes down at his street resemble stained glass: they change colour with the changing drama in the street and, particularly in their framing of the participants below, lend importance to each action in the tragedy. They never forgot that we, the readers, were behind Jacob's shoulder, straining to see, pushing the curtains out of the way at key moments. They never ignored the colours and though they were puzzled (Why's it suddenly gone dark? It was daytime a minute ago) it seemed to me that in contrast to Sendak's *Outside Over There*, they were able to find answers from illustrations that satisfied them. Keeping (1970) claimed that 'children are far more in touch with what is happening and what it's all about when it comes to the art side of it' and it seems to me that he may be right. As a picture-book which encourages children to link episodes, *Through the Window* has few equals. Because we share Jacob's viewpoint we have to give the events a coherence if we are to understand them. The text is composed of Jacob's questions: Why is 'Old Soap' carrying her dog? What did those horses do? but no answers. Answers have to come from the reading of the illustrations; the reader draws inferences, putting cause and effect together to form the most fundamental element of plot structure. The book's story rhythm is also perfect; the opening allows us to move quietly over the view from Jacob's window; the peace is shattered by the stampeding horses and ensuing tragedy; the resolution of the event quietly closes the book. Many interpretations are allowed for; Keeping (1983) himself said 'I didn't say the dog was dead – the reader makes the choice.' We fill in the blanks according to our needs and understanding.

Keeping's control over the story-telling through the illustration is evident in other books where he is both author and illustrator, notably *Joseph's Yard*, *The Garden Shed*, *Railway Passage* and *Wasteground Circus*. All these also make extraordinarily inventive use of colour and line which carry Keeping's strong feelings about the imaginative lives and tough environment of those he chooses to write about – the young and old of Lambeth where he grew up. Whilst pressure groups cry out for books which reflect the life of the inner city child and community, Charles Keeping in these books is doing just that and much else besides.

Across the Atlantic, Keeping's counterpart Ezra Jack Keats was also, in a non-naturalistic style of illustration, reflecting the life of the urban child, but this time of Brooklyn, New York. That many of his stories should show black children is therefore not surprising, but Keats was not black himself and his books have been outlawed in some parts of the United States because he was considered unqualified to portray the black experience. He claimed that he does not attempt that. 'One cannot actually teach people to tolerate each other, to be accepting, to have good manners, to be kind. I don't dream that anyone could do that through a book or in any other way. What I want to do in the "Peter" series is to help children to look at one another and to see one another as human beings. I don't attempt to portray the black experience. The most I can ever do is to open children's eyes. You can't preach. You can't make children make friends. All you can do is reveal people to one another and hope.' (In E. Moss, 1986).

We saw in *Peter's Chair* Keats looking at Peter's coming to terms with the arrival of a new sister. There are other anxieties in the lives of children in Keats's books whether they concern an inability to whistle (*Whistle for Willie*); the threat of large, menacing boys whom you have to outwit (*Goggles*); not having a pet to enter for the pet show other than a germ called Al in a jar (*The Pet Show*); or the problem of a cat who wrecks your games and standing with the little kids (*Hi, Cat!*). In all of these stories we learn of the emotion permeating the kids' lives through the changing colours of their shabby, littered streets and backyards; colours become bright and graffiti glorious when all is well; when one is confused, colours swim together, become murky; when one is frightened, shadows loom and the familiar wall becomes red. Keats's stories show his characters sorting out (frequently through fantasy play) the difficult experiences of growing up and transmuting their surroundings into something alive and manageable. I am particularly impressed by *Apt. 3* which tells the story of a slightly older boy Sam and his discovery of an elderly, blind soul-mate in his apartment block. Sam is pictured lonely at his window, saddened both by driving rain which blurs the whole picture and strange harmonica music which floats up to him. With his brother, down the halls and staircases of his bleak dwelling (thick oil paint represents the plaster walls), he goes in search of the music. Other stories are told both in the lyrical text and the bold, expressionist painting but this distinctive young boy (huge red cap and glowing blue jerkin) eventually finds the music-making blind man and knows that he has found someone who makes tomorrow something to look forward to. Keats represents the music in words: 'He played purples and greys and rain and smoke and the sounds of the night', and through a painting which indicates how the two brothers are lost in the sound: they both lose definition whilst the window behind the blind man glows with brilliant abstract shapes. An optimistic ending, showing the restorative effect of art and imagination. As a matter of interest some of Ezra Jack Keats's books have been produced in dual-language form which suggests that their universality has been recognized by the publishers; on the other hand many of his books are no longer in paperback or are out of print in this country which is strange, considering how welcome they were when they first arrived here and how beautifully told in both words and illustrations they are.

Neither of the two illustrators I am now going to discuss has a large output compared to the established author/illustrators who inevitably demand (and deserve) discussion, but each makes a distinctive contribution both in terms of inducting children into complex meanings and in terms of the specific role of their artwork. The first is Rachel Isadora who, like Keats, is American and like him also is not black but writes and draws in *Ben's Trumpet* of a small black boy who lives opposite the Zig Zag Jazz Club in what could be Harlem in the 1920s. He spends his evenings on the fire escape listening to the jazz and playing his imaginary trumpet. One day his hero from the jazz club passes by. "I like your horn," he says. Joy knows no bounds but is short lived. Sceptical boys mock him and his fantasy melts away. But the trumpeter notices he is no longer 'playing' his horn and senses that a visit to the jazz club and a chance to play a real trumpet is just what he needs.

Rachel Isadora
Ben's Trumpet

One day, Ben is sitting on the steps
and playing his trumpet.
"I like your horn," someone says.

This is a most unusual black and white picture-book, beautifully and thoughtfully conceived as a whole. On the cover the small boy is a black silhouette against the silver silhouette of the trumpeter; the end papers represent white zig-zags of sound across a black background, this arrangement reversed for the title and imprint pages. The first double-page spread gives us the city at night, all heat, winking lights, reflections and fire escapes and the small Ben, still in silhouette raising his 'trumpet' aloft. The period is clinched when we turn the page and see Ben in great tweed cap and herringbone breeches at the door of the club from which bubbles of Charleston-dancing figures float out to form a margin for the picture. We glimpse a decadent limp wrist, a drooping cigarette, a padded shoulder and a trilby hat, recreating with some irony the

Every day on the way home from school, Ben stops by the Zig Zag Jazz Club.

pretensions of the time. Five pages of finely drawn portraits of
the musicians follow, but Ben's hero appears no less than six
times in a crescendo of sound, white lines multiplying till they
explode off the page. The double-page spread of Ben return-
ing home filled with the rhythms shows the very street
responding to Ben's music, bending and curving around him.
More fine line drawings show us Ben's playing going
unnoticed at home by his pre-occupied family. I was happy to
read of Errol Lloyd's (the black illustrator of *My Brother Sean*
and *Nini at Carnival*, books whose painterly illustrations show
positive images of black children in this country) response to
these scenes. 'The book rejoices in the vagaries of black
American ghetto life, without attempting to conceal or roman-
ticise the harsh sleazy realities of what was, after all, a period
of severe economic depression. Nor, on the other hand, is
there too pointed or laboured a reference to the poverty and
deprivation which are the real culprits that stand between Ben
and a real trumpet'. (*Children's Book Bulletin*, No. 5). Three
further illustrations have to be mentioned which chart the
extremes of Ben's mood. The rapture of being noticed by the
trumpeter (the text gives us only 'Ben smiles') is a positive
jungle of crazy, psychedelic, op-art distortions of chequer-
boards, fans, leaves, shells and much else besides. The jeering
boys (across the 'road' which is in fact the gutter of the book!)
leave him hunched beneath his cap, the ghost of a tear
beneath his eye and hard diagonal lines, occupying three
quarters of the page, indicating his wretched state of mind. No
longer living his dream he gazes out at an incomprehensible
fragmented world until eventually the trumpeter comes over,
the pictures settle down and end with a soft, naturalistic drawing expressing the fulfilment of his dream.

I think this is a quite extraordinary book, difficult but holding
out to all readers the importance of aspiration and involving
us intimately with the textures and moods of one small boy's
life at that time. Errol Lloyd wonders whether the pictures,
being so much 'a virtuoso performance', are in danger of
detracting from the central character and theme of the book.
I would maintain they in fact create it. Incidentally, none of the
three reviews I have read of it 'agrees' with my interpretation,
but that is the beauty of reader-response theories.

Satoshi Kitamura, a Japanese illustrator, was apparently on
his way back to Japan, disappointed in his efforts to become

an illustrator in this country, when Klaus Flugge of Andersen
Press invited him to illustrate Hiawyn Oram's text *Angry
Arthur*. At first somewhat unfairly dismissed as a 'pale imitation' of *Where the Wild Things Are* because it also deals with
the anger of childhood, it has become equally sought after by
children because it makes them laugh at the absurdity of

Hiawyn Oram &
Satoshi Kitamura
Angry Arthur

Arthur's tantrum whilst also acknowledging that their bad feelings are legitimate. Here zig-zag lines, hard edges and jagged distortions speak not of the depths of despondency and the heights of ecstasy or of confusion, as they do in *Ben's Trumpet*, but of the enormous destructiveness of Arthur's rage. Small Arthur's mouth, the most expressive zig-zag of

So he did. Very, very angry.
He got so angry that his anger became a stormcloud exploding thunder and lightning and hailstones.

them all, is set in his grim, white face and above tightly clenched fists throughout the ever-increasing chaos. Devastation of room, home, town, planet and universe are depicted against backgrounds which become more lonely and more moody as familiar objects fall away and the deep purple blue of space engulfs him. Leaving Arthur asleep in space may disturb our sense of an appropriate ending for a children's book but the creators of this book have carefully modulated our feelings about this. Firstly the final part of text, ' "Why was I so angry?" he thought. He never did remember. Can you?' sends us straight back to the beginning where we start to notice certain details. The free-standing stove which has escaped from the T.V. Western Arthur was watching turns up again in space along with a space-helmeted Grandmother and her gravity-less ball of knitting wool. Not only does Arthur's anger send 'rooftops, chimneys and church spires' hurtling, but also outsize tipped cigarettes fall from advertising hoardings. These touches of humour and the comforting loyalty of Arthur's cat (details present only in the illustrations) soften what is nevertheless an important story about growing up.

Arthur features again in *In the Attic*, a book which celebrates the richness of imagination in pictures which pay homage to artists such as Piranese, Klee, Magritte and Kandinsky and in a simple, dead-pan text which invites the reader to share the secrets of childhood. Obtuse mothers insist we do not have attics of the mind to explore but then they have not 'found the ladder.' Up the ladder, Kitamura belies the prosaic text and gives us worlds in a grain of sand – or at least in a family of mice, a colony of beetles, a spider and an old engine.

Celebration of the imagination is one theme that runs through Anthony Browne's work. I have looked at two of his books in previous chapters, but in all his picture-books to date, it is evident that he does not regard even his youngest readers as incapable of responding to serious messages if presented entertainingly and honestly. So in *Bear Hunt* the small white bear resourcefully outwits two colonial hunters whose predatory purposes are mocked by surrealist jungle flora and fauna. In *Bear Goes To Town* the same bear rescues various animals bound for slaughter or torture, the implication – carried through the illustrations – being that humanity's treatment of animals has parallels in Nazi persecution. In both these books ingenuity and imagination are the survival strategies in a tough world. *Through a Magic Mirror*, which was in fact Browne's first book where he is clearly learning how to let the illustrations expand the text, also invites us to value our imaginations: look at the world differently, he seems to be saying, then the mundane becomes tolerable. *Look what I've got!* makes it clear, through the series of accidents that befall the possession-obsessed Jeremy (proper names are chosen knowingly by Browne), that again what matters is to do with inner not outer riches. Jeremy is always drawn with eyelids covering his eyes, blind to his own greediness and ignorance and to his friend Sam's kindness. (I owe this obser-

Anthony Browne
Look what I've got!

vation to Jane Doonan, 1986A.) The jumpers holding hands in the illustration perhaps hint at the friendship which could be between the boys if only Jeremy would open his eyes. In *Gorilla* and *The Visitors who came to Stay* Browne tells of loneliness and the adaptations we all need to make and of how life holds surprises for the open-minded. Though he shows single-parent families in these two books there is no labouring of this situation. *Willy the Wimp* and *Willy the Champ* show Browne's favourite animal character learning that aspirations need to be wisely channelled and that natural instincts can be relied upon. These two books which in many ways are modern fables, combining serious messages with humorous and endlessly reverberating visual detail, are not unproblematic. One teacher I spoke to is excluding these books from her classroom because Willy and Milly's faces appear to be significantly paler than the faces of the suburban gorilla gang. Handling the latent racism that readings of these books arouse is something this teacher is not prepared to face. Other teachers are unhappy about the cult of the macho male evident in the two books. Despite aggressive masculinity being both mocked and found wanting the images are so powerful that only they are remembered and not Willy's gentleness. We are not yet ready to accept 'wimp' as a positive attribute. *A Walk in the Park* in both language and images is an exposé of the class divisions in our society which are bridged only by children and animals. Charles and Smudge, their dogs Victoria and Albert, have wonderful fun in a surreal park whilst their respective parents, Mrs Smythe and Mr Smith, 'look the other way' and learn nothing. *Piggybook* as we have seen tackles male chauvinist piggery through images which spell out the metaphor, but maybe some adults will not accept the optimism of the ending, nor do I think the mother's abdication will escape criticism from other quarters. *Hansel and Gretel*, which Anthony Browne has illustrated very thoughtfully, also disturbs some readers who find the contemporary setting (family poverty is clearly linked to maternal extravagance on cosmetics, hair-dos and leopard-skin coat) and the mother/witch fusion too uncomfortable, but it *is* one of the more terrifying fairy tales and Browne interprets it in a classic Freudian way, showing children how to stand on their own feet despite parental inadequacy. His illustrations are full of symbolism; motifs of birds on the one hand and bars and

Anthony Browne
Hansel and Gretel

cages on the other represent, respectively, progression and regression on Hansel and Gretel's part. The numerous black triangles which we meet in juxtaposition to the step-mother alert us to the role she also plays as witch. Jane Doonan, who has made a 14,000 word special study of Browne's *Hansel and Gretel*, is right, I am sure, in saying that children know that real families are not as they are commonly portrayed in popular culture – mothers staying twenty-seven for ever, with never a cross word. Anthony Browne offers them a deeper kind of fantasy against which to measure their experience and feelings.

Anthony Browne is doing something very special in British classrooms. His characteristic placing of familiar objects in unexpected places lures children into his books and there, as well as laughing, they are enabled to make discoveries about the nature of society, human relationships, the human spirit and moral values.

There are three other illustrators who have also changed the face of picture-books, all in distinctively different ways but all telling the child, through pictures that do their own talking and words that sometimes speak quite plainly, that books are a place to find significant stories about life.

One cannot underestimate the role that Raymond Briggs's comic strip books could play in the making of a reader. In Chapter 3 we saw how the youngest children can 'tell' the story of *The Snowman*, feeling through both characters and learning the shaping of the story where key moments are signified through enlarged frames and 'viewing' speed is carefully regulated so that, for instance, we race through the penultimate frames but linger on the very last picture. In all his gently ironic books there is this same mastery of the comic strip form.

There is much anxiety amongst adults about comic material for children for very differing reasons. Elaine Moss (1986) reports that Walter Benjamin in the 1930s wondered whether any child 'raised in the howling blizzard of signals would ever find his way back into the exacting silence of a book,' and that Bettina Hürlimann asked in 1959 if 'picture and bubble language would succeed in halting the literature of the future'. Peter Dickinson felt the need to come to the defence of comics arguing, amongst other things, that comic-reading makes one feel part of a group; that it keeps one in touch with the popular culture of one's time; that it gives one a feeling of autonomy; that it provides escape-routes; that it provides 'roughage' from which discrimination grows (in Fox *et al* 1976). What he might have added is that comics, like other 'rubbish' whether Enid Blyton or mystery stories generally, teach important literary conventions in effective if simple ways. Above all else they involve readers in the 'active process of simultaneous anticipation of the unknown yet to come and retrospection about what has already occurred' (Iser, 1978). As Fred Inglis (1981), one of many who now 'own up' to their reading of comics in youth, writes, 'We knew what was in them and yet anything might be in them.'

Raymond Briggs, as a narrative illustrator in the comic-strip tradition, does all of that but unlike the stories in the average comic or even in the *Tintin*, *Asterix*, and *Rupert Bear* series which he admires, his stories involve us even whilst making us smile in a contemplation of some of the most serious and momentous aspects of existence. *When the Wind Blows* which 'takes us to a place no picture book has ever taken us before' (*New York Times*) is the obvious example of this but even in *Father Christmas* and *Father Christmas goes on Holiday* there is a pathos as well as humour and we find there, as well as in *Fungus the Bogeyman* and *Gentleman Jim*, the questioning of the purpose of our existence that can include gentle swipes at the consumer society, bureaucracy, education and civilization itself. And of course Raymond Briggs's characters are the very opposite of the rough, omnipotent dare-devil heroes of the average comic. And whilst comic art-work is often extraordinarily sophisticated, in Briggs's books the control over the form is complete. Stories often start with significant end-papers (green marbling for *Fungus*, bleakest black for *When the Wind Blows*) and important title pages (Jim reads of impending war in the library's *Times* under a sombre notice SILENCE); speech bubbles break frame at significant moments; dreams, wildest fantasies and memories are indicated by letting them break extravagantly through the straightforward story frames; changing colours and cross-sectioning can mark passage of time or seasons, movement and progression generally. In *When the Wind Blows*, which takes an unflinching look at nuclear destruction, Briggs makes stupendous use of double-page spreads to depict the encroaching dangers of rocket, planes and submarine, heightening the suspense as we watch Jim and Hilda in hundreds of smaller frames prepare with heart-breaking optimism for The Bomb. The 'blinding flash' must be one of the most eloquent empty pages in the whole of literature. Though there is nothing on the page except the palest pink fringe, no reader turns straight over; everybody at this point looks into their own most dreaded fantasy.

Whilst I have focused on Briggs's illustrative art, again and again one is amazed also at the inventive writing his books give us. Much is done through under-statement, the satirist's most important weapon; occasionally, so that perhaps all readers whatever their age should not fail to understand, his characters look straight out at us, the readers, whilst they declare 'I am, yet what I am who knows. I am the self-consumer of my woes' (*Fungus*), 'I bet it's all to do with Education – that's what it is . . .' (*Gentleman Jim*), and 'After all, it will all be over in a flash' (*When the Wind Blows*). The subtlety of his scripts has disconcerted those who want to pigeon-hole his books as suitable only above a certain age; in fact I suspect that many young readers are introduced to irony and pathos for the first time in Briggs's poignant comic-strips.

Certainly it is young children who will face squarely the issues in some of David McKee's books. I have looked at *Not Now, Bernard* which whilst immensely popular with children is certainly not the cheerful and reassuring read that McKee's *King Rollo* books are. *Tusk, Tusk* is even more reverberating. Aggressive black and white elephants (whose trunks can become accusatory fingers, clenched fists, cannons, revolvers) battle until they destroy each other; the grandchildren of the peace loving elephants who had avoided this warfare emerge later from the jungle, grey in colour. Those who have criticized this book (Americans said they had enough of a colour problem without *Tusk, Tusk*, and Germans, so McKee claims, said he was talking about creating a master race) may have failed to perceive the significance of McKee's final, typically equivocal, illustration and its resonant postscript 'But recently the little ears and the big ears have been giving each other strange looks.' To see the book as proposing a melting-pot solution to racial problems is to ignore its passionate message that unless we accept differences of all kinds we will all end up dead. The small cameo which opens the book is tellingly captioned "Vive la différence." Funny, amazingly versatile

David McKee
Tusk, Tusk

elephants who live amongst equally expressive birds in a jungle that becomes literally concrete at times take children effortlessly through this serious morality tale.

Michael Foreman's books are well known for their social, political and moral themes. Pacifism (*The Two Giants; Moose*), inequality *(War and Peas)*, conservation (*Dinosaurs and all that Rubbish*), gender stereotyping (*All the King's Horses*), existentialism (*Panda's Puzzle*) are dealt with in allegorical form made yet more accessible through illustration that uses colour wash, line and page layout to suggest mood, humour and drama. One of his more recent picture-books, *Land of Dreams*, is particularly delightful to discuss here because Foreman, in picture-book form, is arguing the case for illustration in children's books. That needs explaining. The text tells of an old man and a boy who live high above the world in snowy mountains (Foreman conceived the idea for this book after a visit to the Himalayas) where the world's unfinished dreams and lost hopes finally come to rest. In this scrapyard, the pair work to reassemble the shape of dreams so that the world can smile again. A giant arrives bemoaning the fact that he is no longer a powerful imaginative symbol for the world. "In the old days . . . I used to stomp about in the dreams of everyone." The old man and the boy help him to uncover his self image from the snow and dream and giant leave together to inhabit the great collective unconscious once more. The old man muses on whether the young boy will one day leave to find *his* dream, but the boy, smiling as he turns over in bed, has all the dreams he needs.

As the text stands, it argues the case for the importance of the imagination. Add the illustrations and the imagination is embodied in images from film, television, mythology, history, literature and most particularly from children's books. There, through the cold blue mountain-air, is a ghostly galleon tossed upon cloudy seas; there, half-buried in a snow drift, is a plumed helmet and an Arthurian sword. Turn the pages and Humpty-Dumpty, Babar, White Rabbit, Cupid, the Clockwork Soldier, Rupert Bear, Hiawatha, the Statue of Liberty, Moby Dick, Punch, the Leaning Tower of Pisa, Noah's Ark, Joan of Arc, Icarus, dinosaurs, daleks, spacemen, pharaohs, pagodas, the onion domes of Moscow, not to mention several 'quotations' from Foreman's own work, wait to re-enter our inner world. What wonderful visual intertextuality!

As in all Foreman's books there is close attention to colour – here all is swirling blues, whites and pinks which create a cold but strangely soft and dreamlike world. He has made extraordinary use of a thick embossed paper so that the very texture of the snow can be 'felt'. Space is equally thoughtfully handled – stretches of snow-covered mountain ranges fill the pages and become quite abstract at the beginning and end of the book, melting in and out of the boy's bedding to further underpin the theme of imagination's limitless sweeps. There is one quite special moment, told only in the visual text. The form that the giant's recovered dream takes is known only through the pictures – we *see* that it is a massive version of himself, the text only ever describing it as a dream. But even before the man and the boy realize what lies under the top five hundred feet of the highest mountain, the giant finds and joyously holds aloft a vast snow-covered heart. Unmentioned in the text, this heart now gives the reader direct access to the point Foreman so often makes in his work – that humanity must think more with its heart. It is a theme present in Foreman's earliest books – the dinosaur says to the bowler-hatted bureaucrat in his space-suit, "If you had been ruled by your heart instead of your head, you would not have destroyed this paradise before" (*Dinosaurs and all that Rubbish*). But in *Land of Dreams* the image is there as a symbol to be understood without supportive text, all the more powerful because we have to bring meaning to it.

The books I have discussed in this Chapter are not unique. Many others exist including several of those mentioned in earlier chapters which would equally demonstrate the potentially humanizing power of art. But the ones I have isolated all extend generous invitations to the child to enter their imaginary worlds. They all share a belief that children want to think as well as to laugh. They all have an ability to leave resonating images in the mind around which meanings can grow long after the book is put down. The 'implied reader' of these books has proved problematic for many a critic, parent and teacher: are an ice-baby, or a dead dog, a leopard-skin-coated step-mother or a gambling father, nuclear flashes or dead elephants icons that we want to give to children? Answers to these questions will continue to divide the adult world. Children respond to the respect which these serious author/illustrators accord them and learn how to read the important messages that books can bring.

The Way Ahead

In conclusion, through a close look at *Granpa* by John Burningham, I want to recapitulate on several issues connected with illustration and point to new areas that indicate how much more exploration there is to be done.

Granpa tells, through economical pictures and apparently random scraps of text, of the joys and sorrows in a friendship between a small girl and her grandfather which comes to an end with the old man's death, symbolized poignantly by the child gazing across the blank space of the page to her grandfather's empty chair. Picture-books which tell of death usually deal with the death of an animal – one thinks of Viorst's *The Tenth Good Thing About Barney* and Keeping's *Through the Window*. Burningham, like Raymond Briggs, does not eschew the subject of human death, though like Tomie de Paola in *Nana Upstairs, Nana Downstairs* he writes of the death of an old person. This allows the reader to reflect both on its inevitability and on the full life that has been lead. In Burningham's book, the sepia drawings below the text give us flashbacks to Granpa's youth; the passing of the seasons (the book reaches winter when Granpa dies) suggests a complete life; and the final picture of the child pushing her pram up a windy hill suggests continuing life. The book speaks in sorrowful but not distraught tones.

Nevertheless many adults are troubled by the theme. Coupled with the seemingly inconsequential text, they feel it makes the book impenetrable to the 'average' child. 'The identity of such a book's consumer is obscure' writes Julia Briggs in *The Times Literary Supplement* of 30.11.84. 'Young readers will grasp its meanings intuitively, if at all.' This is to reckon without the full force of the illustrations. What happens with a complex book like this is that the illustrations have their own way of both ensuring involvement and creating understanding. Burningham's pictures, held in the memory to be pursued perhaps even in dreams, hold the solution to the book's enigmas. The child who may not instantly bring understanding to the empty chair may come back the next day to link it with the earlier illustration of a pale Grandfather, rug over his knees, pills to hand. The next day, the skating where Granpa nearly slips may also be understood in its suggestion of frailty. Perhaps then the child will wonder about the journey to Africa which the little girl plans for her granpa as they watch television together. The sepia drawing shows a ship sailing towards a last sunset. Every illustration is fed by an earlier or later one: Burningham, if we let him, teaches us how to bring meaning to the book.

It is possible that adults anticipate difficulty with this book on children's behalf because to some extent the traditions out of which it springs are very recent. The scraps of text are entirely in dialogue, grandfather's words in bold type, his grand-daughter's in italics. Much of what they say seems to be non-sequiturs. Adults may hear echoes of Pinter but for the child reader it is familiarity with television, where all stories come in pictures and dialogue, that gives the book its coherence. The book proceeds in a televisual way: the episodes are short and 'cut' in medias res. The television-trained child will not expect sequence but will be looking for a holding frame. The sepia annotations serve several purposes all well-known from the television screen: close-ups of the greenhouse shelf, the garden pond and the medicine bottle; flashbacks to Granpa's boyhood sing-songs, cream teas and toboggan runs; sudden visions of an ultra-feminine teddy bear and the capture of a whale; glimpses of a croquet mallet lying long neglected in a garden shed; the freeze-frame of the symbolic ship on the horizon. As to the text, the child reader will have to work, but familiarity with the one-liners of television will help with the filling in of the sometimes differing wave-length conversations. Where the child might be ignorant (is 'One man went to mow' a song in everyone's culture?), the operatic gestures in the illustrations tell us that both Granpa and the little girl are singing. We can then surmise from the sepia drawing that Granpa learnt this song in an Edwardian parlour in his youth. The sudden intrusion of lines from the Noah story are illuminated when we see Granpa in an upstairs window, clearly choosing to read an appropriate story whilst the rain lashes down. The ability to allow pictures to explain the text can be developed by television viewing and may well explain the relative ease with which this television generation understands

John Burningham
Granpa

this book. It is Bruner (1984) who said 'television could in fact be used as an ancillary to the teaching of reading'. Maybe it is not co-incidental that Burningham gives Granpa his last moment in front of a television. This is not to forget the one inestimable advantage that the picture-book has over television and that is the reader's freedom to move backwards and forwards over the text as is clearly necessary in *Granpa*.

There is another key which unlocks *Granpa* which is often lost to adults who assume that the book is beyond children's understanding. Children, we know, can find in reading a 'specifically good kind of play, less trouble than dressing up but just as exciting for imagining you are someone else and

somewhere else' (M. Meek, 1982). In many of the books I
have discussed in earlier chapters there is a clear relation
between the attention children will give to the illustrations and
their experience of imaginative play. In play, children learn 'to
sever thought from object' (Vygotsky, 1978) and then act
according to the meaning so that, for instance, the pictures
seen flat in a book can be made to 'mean' just as Vygotsky's
stick can 'mean' a horse. Kenneth Grahame, as will be clear
from the extracts heading earlier chapters, clearly 'entered'
illustrations and felt himself playing a role with other characters. But there is a more direct application of the child's
experience of play to the illustrations in *Granpa* (and in many

books such as *The Sign on Rosie's Door* and *Me and my Flying Machine*). The life of the imagination, of make-believe, which merges with reality so easily in childhood, gives direct access to understanding of, for instance, the double-page spread in *Granpa* where the grandfather's quite reasonable assumption that the brown soil which he is 'eating' is chocolate ice-cream draws severe correction from the small girl: "It's not chocolate, it's strawberry." Many other openings of *Granpa* can be understood only if one is close to the world of the child, a world where the after-life of the worm and the gender of a toy bear exist as concerns alongside the possibility of one's home becoming a modern Noah's ark or of hooking a whale

That was not a nice thing

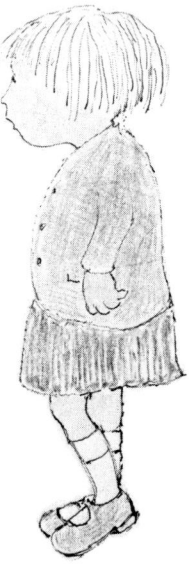

in the local river, or the impossibility of imagining that the sea-side could ever pall or that Granpa could have once been a baby. Burningham's reflection of the child's inner world meets the reader's first-hand experience of fantasy, hope and speculation. The child who has a full experience of imaginative play may be better equipped to understand than many an adult. This is one area which needs further investigation.

Another area which I have touched upon only incidentally and which needs much more research is the role of the adult in the sharing of picture-books with children. The Cragos, in their observations of their daughter's growth as a reader (1976), eschewed intervention and documented very care-

to say to Granpa.

fully Anna's comments and questions about books over a period of time concluding that adult and child are not so far apart in their responses, only in their capacity to make those responses explicit. Important findings were that the more time Anna had to gaze at a particular picture the more likely she was to volunteer comment and that multiple readings developed her ability to link picture and text and picture and picture. This is part of classroom findings also. 'Teachers recognized that children needed time for initial reactions to deepen into more profound responses, so they reintroduced the children to books after a period of weeks or months had passed and children might bring new experiences to their repeated readings' (Kiefer, 1985). By contrast, Marilyn Cochran-Smith (1984) studied story-time in a nursery school and recorded the very active role that adult story-readers play during this time, which she described as 'natural' story reading as opposed to the Cragos' 'experimental sessions'. By focusing on interactive patterns, Cochran-Smith is certainly able to confirm the central role that the achievement of labelling plays with its turn-taking rules. The 'unilateral sense-making of decontextualized storybooks' which takes place in library hour she tends to feel gives no model to the child listener of how to 'take' from texts. She claims that children for instance 'needed to be helped to realize that in-between a picture of a boy headed menacingly towards a snowman and one of the base of the snowman, the snowman had been knocked down'. It was the adult's role to point out the way in which the pictured actions are related to one another.

Between these two extremes I am sure there can be a happy medium. If we return to *Granpa*, any sensitive adult will probably want to 'scaffold' the entry into the book in many ways, relating the book to the known experiences of the child and directing the child to discover answers to questions within the text. Gordon Wells (1985) is in no doubt about the facilitating role of the adult: 'Where stories are related to children's own experiences and they are encouraged to reflect upon and ask questions about the events that occur, their causes, consequences and significance, not only are their inner representations of the world enriched but also their awareness of the ways in which language can be used in operating on these representations is enhanced.'

However, it is surely a mis-reading of Iser for Marilyn Cochran-Smith to approve of teachers doing so much of children's gap-filling for them. No adult should *tell* a child that Granpa and grand-daughter have quarrelled when we see them back to back after their little tiff. Their isolation in the vast emptiness of a double-page spread, their puzzled demeanours allow the meanings to grow if, as the Cragos note, the child is given time. All the taped and video-ed evidence is that teachers intervene too much and do not allow literature to do its own work. I have tried to show how illustrations play their part in the process.

What I think Cochran-Smith does value rightly is the importance of adult readers' intonation, facial expression, head movements. 'The prosodic and paralinguistic accompaniment provides a great deal of information in addition to that conveyed by lexical and syntactic features of written text.' I am reminded of how much my secondary school struggling readers were helped by dramatic renderings of text and by any enactments that one found oneself employing. 'The dramatic story, the personal narrative full of stance and scenario' as Bruner (1984) describes the ideal reading text needs to be given as much intrinsic support as the teller can muster. Different intonation will actually alter interpretation of course. I talk about the small girl in *Granpa* reproving her grandfather for incorrect identification of the ice cream because I 'hear' her speaking with a snap in her voice. Another reader may whisper her words changing the small child from a dictator to a gentle collaborator. Burningham's illustrations are not so precise that differing readings of this nature cannot be obtained.

We do not want to put our young readers into laboratories with their picture-books but neither do we want to have adults rob them of their essential need to do 'quite half the labour'. Why Dorothy White's record (1956) of her daughter's reading growth has so much to offer is that it combines a splendid mixture of a parent's warm curiosity about her child's development and individuality, a librarian's respect and enthusiasm for the books' power to teach and not too much of the teacher's need to interfere.

The last area I wish to isolate for further investigation is the extent to which illustrations need to reflect the heterogeneous nature of their audience. Whilst the 'secondary world' keeps us there, if it does, because of its emotional truth, there is a shortage of illustrated books which give back a physical verisimilitude to their readers. Picture-books commonly display a middle-class environment. *Granpa* is not immune in that respect as Grandfather lives in an extraordinarily grand house with conservatory and spacious garden, not unlike Mr Gumpy's, as children are quick to point out. At least Burningham has a girl in his cast. It came as quite a shock to realize that over two thirds of the main protagonists in the illustrations I examined were male. The situation was similar in Kenneth Grahame's time – 'Of course the girls fared badly in this book and it was not surprising that they preferred the 'Pilgrim's Progress' (for instance), where women had a fair show, and there was generally enough of 'em to go round; or a good fairy story, wherein princesses met with a healthy appreciation.' (1898)

When it comes to ethnicity, the black or brown protagonist is still rare. As I have indicated earlier, certain pressures prevent white illustrators presenting the black experience. Involving minority groups in book creation is the way ahead. Muriel Whitaker (1975) writes of interesting developments in Canada where involvement of Indian and Inuit artists is not only removing the stereotype of American 'bad guy' Indians brandishing tomahawks and taking scalps but is also introducing readers to the artistic techniques of the Pacific Northwest totem poles, Eastern pictographs and Arctic soapstone sculptures and prints.

What effect these imbalances may have on readers needs further elucidation and what might be done about it is yet another matter. It is certainly no solution to write formula stories about children of mixed race marriages whose mothers work and whose unemployed fathers happily child-mind, awaiting the West Indian milkman and entertaining the Asian neighbour before mother arrives home bearing a present of a non-sexist doctor's dressing-up outfit. I draw a veil over the title of this recently published 'book'. If we want fathers in caring roles we can turn for instance to Louis Baum's *I want to see the Moon* or Browne and McAfee's *The Visitors who came to Stay* or Gabrielle Vincent's 'Ernest and Celestine' books.

Some serious work has been done by Barrie Wade (1986) on how reading scheme illustrations reinforce crude messages about reading itself. 'Story books are for girls; boys read comics; men read newspapers' or so the pictures tell us. More awareness of pervasive messages like these needs to be fostered. At least Willy the Wimp 'liked to read'!

It is my conviction that picture-books have an underestimated power to communicate the essential elements of narrative shape and that readers young and old are recruited by picture-books to engage with the emotional and intellectual meanings that characterize all good reading experiences. It is for somebody trained in the art world to judge whether children's artistic education is furthered by the infinite variety of artwork they meet in picture-books. Ruskin certainly thought so. In 1883 he wrote, 'In the matter of pictures, fortune indeed has so far favoured the child that he may be said to be something of an art critic ere he leaves the cradle.' He went on to say 'Nursery literature is a thing of the past; nursery art shows radiant and delightful in its room.' I think if he had witnessed the modern picture-book he would have felt that nursery literature was no longer in any danger, that, indeed, it had an essential role to play in the teaching of the literary conventions that all readers operate throughout their lives.

Bibliography 1. – *Children's Books*

AHLBERG, Allan and Janet
    Burglar Bill   Heinemann 1973
    Each Peach Pear Plum   Viking Kestrel 1978
    Peepo   Viking Kestrel 1981

ANNO, Mitsumasa
    Anno's Journey   Bodley Head 1978

ARDIZZONE, Edward
    Little Tim and the Brave Sea Captain   Viking Kestrel (New Edition 1982)

BAUM, Louis & DALY, Nikki
    I want to see the Moon   Bodley Head 1984

BEMELMANS, Ludwig
    Madeline   Andre Deutsch 1952

BERNADETTE
    Cinderella   J M Dent 1979

BRIGGS, Raymond
    The Elephant and the Bad Baby
       (with Elfrida Vipont)   Hamish Hamilton 1969
    Father Christmas   Hamish Hamilton 1973
    Father Christmas Goes on Holiday   Hamish Hamilton 1975
    Fungus the Bogeyman   Hamish Hamilton 1977
    The Snowman   Hamish Hamilton 1978
    Gentleman Jim   Hamish Hamilton 1980
    When the Wind Blows   Hamish Hamilton 1982

BROWN, Ruth
    A Dark Dark Tale   Andersen Press 1981

BROWNE, Anthony
    Through the Magic Mirror   Hamish Hamilton 1976
    A Walk in the Park   Hamish Hamilton 1977
    Bear Hunt   Hamish Hamilton 1979
    Look what I've got!   Julia MacRae Books 1980
    Hansel and Gretel   Julia MacRae Books 1981
    Bear Goes to Town   Hamish Hamilton 1982
    Gorilla   Julia MacRae Books 1983
    Willy the Wimp   Julia MacRae Books 1984
    Willy the Champ   Julia MacRae Books 1985
    The Visitors who came to Stay
       (with Annalena McAfee)   Hamish Hamilton 1985
    Piggybook   Julia MacRae Books 1986

BRUNA, Dick
    The king   Methuen 1964

BURNINGHAM, John
    Mr. Gumpy's Outing   Jonathan Cape 1970
    Mr. Gumpy's Motor Car   Jonathan Cape 1973
    Come away from the water, Shirley   Jonathan Cape 1977
    Time to get out of the bath, Shirley   Jonathan Cape 1978
    Granpa   Jonathan Cape 1984

CALDECOTT, Randolph
    Bye Baby Bunting   Routledge c.1870

CARROLL, Lewis
    Alice in Wonderland

    illustrators:

    TENNIEL, John   Macmillan 1865
    RACKHAM, Arthur   Heinemann 1907
    STEADMAN, Ralph   A. Dobson 1967
    KALINOVSKY, Genadij   Detskaya Literatura 1977

CUTLER, Ivor & OXENBURY, Helen
    Meal One   Heinemann 1971

FLACK, Marjorie & WEISE, Kurt
    The Story of Ping   Bodley Head 1935

FOREMAN, Michael
    The Two Giants   Hodder & Stoughton 1967
    Dinosaurs and all that Rubbish   Hamish Hamilton 1972
    War and Peas   Hamish Hamilton 1974
    Moose   Hamish Hamilton 1975
    All the King's Horses   Hamish Hamilton 1976
    Panda's Puzzle   Hamish Hamilton 1977
    Land of Dreams   Andersen Press 1982

GANLY, Helen
    Jyoti's Journey   Andre Deutsch 1986

GRAHAME, Kenneth & SHEPARD, Ernest H.
    The Wind in the Willows   Methuen 1908

HALES, Kathleen
    Orlando the Marmalade Cat   Country Life 1938

HEIDE, Florence Parry & GOREY, Edmund
    The Shrinking of Treehorn   Viking Kestrel 1975

HERRMANN, Frank & HIM, George
    The Giant Alexander   Methuen 1964

HOBAN, Russell & BLAKE, Quentin
    How Tom beat Captain Najork and his
        Hired Sportsmen   Jonathan Cape 1974

HERGÉ
        The Adventures of Tintin   Methuen 1966

HUGHES, Shirley
        Up and Up   Bodley Head 1979
        Alfie Gets in First   Bodley Head 1981

HUTCHINS, Pat
        Rosie's Walk   Bodley Head 1968
        Changes, Changes   Bodley Head 1971
        Titch   Bodley Head 1972
        You'll Soon Grow into Them, Titch   Bodley Head 1972

INNOCENTI, Roberto
        Rose Blanche   Jonathan Cape 1985

ISADORA, Rachel
        Ben's Trumpet   Angus & Robertson 1980

KEATS, Ezra Jack
        Whistle for Willie   Bodley Head 1966
        Peter's Chair   Bodley Head 1968
        Goggles   Bodley Head 1970
        Hi, Cat!   Bodley Head 1971
        Apt. 3   Hamish Hamilton 1971
        The Pet Show   Hamish Hamilton 1972

KEEPING, Charles
        Joseph's Yard   Oxford 1969
        Through the Window   Oxford 1970
        The Garden Shed   Oxford 1971
        Wasteground Circus   Oxford 1972
        Railway Passage   Oxford 1974
        Inter-City   Oxford 1977
        River   Oxford 1978
        The Highwayman   Oxford 1981
        Beowulf   Oxford 1982
        Sammy Streetsinger   Oxford 1984
        The Wedding Ghost   Oxford 1985
        The Lady of Shalott   Oxford 1986

LE CAIN, Errol
        Cinderella   Penguin 1977

LIONNI, Leo
        Frederick   Andersen Press 1971

LLOYD, Errol
        My Brother Sean
           (with Petronella Breinburg)   Bodley Head 1973
        Nini at Carnival   Bodley Head 1978

MARIS, Ron
        My book   Julia MacRae Books 1983

MAYER, Mercer (ill.) & MAYER, Marianne
    Me and my Flying Machine   Collins 1973
    Beauty and the Beast   Four Winds Press N.Y. 1978

McKEE, David
    Tusk, Tusk   Andersen Press 1978
    Not now, Bernard   Andersen Press 1980
    I Hate My Teddy Bear   Andersen Press 1982

OAKLEY, Graham
    The Church Mouse   Macmillan 1972

ORAM, Hiawyn & KITAMURA, Satoshi
    Angry Arthur   Andersen Press 1982
    In the Attic   Andersen Press 1984

ORMEROD, Jan
    Sunshine   Viking Kestrel 1981

OSBORNE, Eileen & PEARSE, S.B.
    Ameliaranne   Harrap 1940

PAOLA, Tomie de
    Nana Upstairs, Nana Downstairs   Putnam 1973

POTTER, Beatrix
    The Tale of Peter Rabbit   Frederick Warne & Co. 1902

SENDAK, Maurice
    Little Bear
      (with Else Minarik)   World's Work 1957
    The Juniper Tree   Bodley Head 1964
    Where the Wild Things Are   Bodley Head 1967
    Mr. Rabbit and the Lovely Present
      (with Charlotte Zolotow)   Bodley Head 1968
    Higglety Pigglety Pop!   Bodley Head 1969
    The Sign on Rosie's Door   Bodley Head 1969
    Outside Over There   Bodley Head 1981

SPIER, Peter
    The Great Flood   World's Work 1978

STOBBS, William
    Gregory's Dog   Oxford 1984

VINCENT, Gabrielle
    Ernest and Celestine   Julia MacRae Books 1982
    Bravo, Ernest and Celestine   Julia MacRae Books 1982
    Smile Please, Ernest and Celestine Julia MacRae Books 1982

VIORST, Judith & BLEGVAD, Erik
    The Tenth Good Thing About Barney Collins 1972

WAGNER, Jenny & BROOKS, Ron
    John Brown, Rose and the Midnight Cat Viking Kestrel 1977

WILDSMITH, Brian
    Cat on the Mat   Oxford 1982

READING SCHEMES

Oxford Reading Tree   Oxford

Puddle Lane   Ladybird

Story Chest   E. J. Arnold

    In a dark, dark wood (ill. Christine Ross)
    Plop! (ill. Christine Ross)
    The big toe (ill. Martin Bailey)

Ginn 360   Ginn

    Kim Ann and the Yellow Machine (ill. Mercer Mayer)

Open Door   Nelson

    New Boots for the Dragon (ill. David McKee)
    Elephants going to bed (ill. Tony Ross)

Bibliography 2. – Academic Books and Articles

BENTON, Michael — 'Children's Response to Stories', *Children's Literature in Education*, Vol. 10, No. 2, Summer 1979 New York: Agathon Press Inc.

BENTON, Michael & FOX, Geoff — *Teaching Literature 9–14*, Oxford University Press 1985.

BERRIDGE, Celia — 'Taking a good look at Picture Books', *Signal 36*, September 1981.

BETTELHEIM, Bruno — *The Uses of Enchantment: The Meaning and Importance of Fairy Tales*, London: Thames & Hudson 1976.

BRITTON, James — *Language and Learning*, London: Allen Lane 1970

BRUNER, Jerome — 'Language, Mind and Reading', in *Awakening to Literacy*, eds. Goelman, A., Oberg, A. & Smith, F., London: Heinemann 1984.

CHAMBERS, Aidan — 'The Child's Changing Story', *Signal 40*, January 1983.
Booktalk, London: The Bodley Head 1985.

CHATMAN, Seymour — *Story and discourse: Narrative Structure in Fiction and Film*, Cornell University Press 1978.

CHORAO, Kay — 'A Delayed Reply: Illustration and the Imagination', *Horn Book Magazine*, August 1979

COCHRAN-SMITH, M. — *The Making of a Reader*, Norwood N. J.: Ablex, 1984.

COMENIUS, A. J. (trans Charles Hoole 1777) — *Orbis Sensualium Pictus*

COTT, Jonathan (ed.) — *Victorian Color Picture Books*, London: Allen Lane 1984.

CRAGO, H. & M. — 'The untrained eye? A pre-school child explores Felix Hoffman's Rapunzel.' *Children's Literature in Education*, No. 22 Autumn 1976 New York: Agathon Press Inc.

CULLER, Jonathan — *The Pursuit of Signs*, London: Routledge & Kegan Paul 1978.

DE LUCA, Geraldine — 'Exploring the levels of Childhood: The Allegorical Sensibility of Maurice Sendak', in *Children's Literature*, Vol. 12, Yale University Press 1984.

DICKINSON, Peter — 'A Defence of Rubbish', in *Writers, Critics and Children*, ed. Fox, G. et al, Heinemann 1976.

DIXON, Bob — *Now Read On*, Pluto 1982.

DONALDSON, M. — *Children's Minds*, Fontana 1978.

DOONAN, Jane — 'Talking Pictures: A new look at Hansel & Gretel', *Signal 42*, September 1983.

'The object lesson: picture books of Anthony Browne' in *Word & Image*, ed. P. Hollindale, Taylor & Francis 1986.

'Outside over there: A Journey in Style', (Part one), *Signal 50*, May 1986.

EGOFF, Sheila STUBBS, G. T. and ASHLEY, L. F. (eds.) — *Only Connect: Readings on Children's Literature*, Toronto: Oxford University Press 1969

FOX, Geoff et al — *Writers, Critics and Children*, London: Heinemann 1976.

FRY, Donald — *Children talk about books*, Oxford University Press 1985.

GARDNER, Howard — *Art, Mind and Brain*, Basic Books 1982.

GOODMAN, K. S. — 'Analysis of Oral Reading Miscues: Applied Psycholinguistics', *Reading Research Quarterly*, Fall 1969.

GOODMAN, Paul — *The Structure of Literature*, University of Chicago 1954.

GRAHAME, Kenneth — *Dream Days (Essays of Childhood)*, John Lane 1898, republished Paul Harris 1983.

HARIES, A., DISKI, R., and BROWN, A. — *The Child is not Dead*. ILEA and British Defence and Aid Fund 1986

HART, Joan and RICHARDSON, J. A. — *Books for the Retarded Reader*, Benn 1971

HUGHES, Shirley — 'Word and Image' in *Only the best is good enough*, (Woodfield lectures on children's literature), ed. Fearn, M., London: Rosendale Press 1985.

INGLIS, Fred — *The Promise of Happiness*, Cambridge University Press 1981.

ISER, Wolfgang — *The Implied Reader*, Johns Hopkins University Press 1974

The Act of Reading, London: Routledge & Kegan Paul 1978.

KEEPING, Charles — 'Illustration in children's books', *Children's Literature in Education*, No. 1 March 1970 Ward Lock Educational

In Seminar Proceedings, Loughborough, 1983.

KIEFER, Barbara — 'Looking Beyond Picture Book References', *Horn Book Magazine*, Vol. LXI, No. 6, November/December 1985.

LANES, Selma	*The Art of Maurice Sendak*, New York: Abrams 1984
LANGER, Susanne	*Feeling and Form*, London: Routledge & Kegan Paul 1953.
LURIE, Alison	*A Language of Clothes*, Heinemann 1981
MEEK, Margaret, WARLOW, A. and BARTON, G. (eds.)	*The Cool Web: The Pattern of Children's Reading*, London: The Bodley Head 1977.
MEEK, Margaret	*Learning to Read*, London: The Bodley Head 1982
MOSS, Elaine	*Part of the Pattern*, London: The Bodley Head 1986.
NINIO, A. and BRUNER, J.	'The Achievement and Antecedents of Labelling', *Journal of Child Language*, No. 5, 1978
RUSKIN, John	*Magazine of Art*, VI, 1883.
SAMUELS, S. J.	'Effects of pictures on learning to read, comprehension and attitude', *Review of Educational Research*, Vol. 40, 1970.
SCHALLERT, D. L.	'The Role of Illustrations in Reading Comprehension', in *Theoretical Issues in Reading Comprehension*, ed. Spiro, R. J. et al, L. Erlbaum, U.S., 1980.
SMERDON, Gerald	'Children's Preferences in illustration', *Children's Literature in Education*, No. 20 Spring 1976 New York: Agathon Press Inc.
STEIG, Michael	'Reading Outside Over There', in *Children's Literature*, Vol. 13, Yale University Press 1985.
TOLKIEN, J. R. R.	*Tree and Leaf*, London: Allen & Unwin 1964.
TUCKER, Nicholas	'Edward Ardizzone', *Children's Literature in Education*, No. 3 November 1970 Ward Lock Educational
VYGOTSKY, L. S.	*Mind in Society*, Harvard University Press 1978
WADE, Barrie	'A Picture of Reading', *Education Review*, Vol. 38, 1986.
WELLS, Gordon	*Language, Learning and Education*, NFER, Nelson 1985.
WERNER, Craig	'A Blind Child's View of Children's Literature' in *Children's Literature*, Vol. 12, Yale University Press 1984.
WHITAKER, Muriel	'Louder Than Words: the Didactic use of Illustration in Books for Children', *Children's Literature in Education*, No. 16 Spring 1975 New York: Agathon Press Inc.
WHITE, Dorothy	*Books Before Five*, New Zealand Council for Educational Research 1956.

Acknowledgements

Judith Graham and NATE wish to thank the following publishers and artists for permission to use their work:

Penguin Books Ltd, Jenny Wagner and Ron Brooks for text and illustrations from *John Brown, Rose and the Midnight Cat* © 1977 Jenny Wagner and Ron Brooks; and Jan Ormerod for illustrations from *Sunshine* © 1981 Jan Ormerod; and Edward Ardizzone for illustrations from *Little Tim and the Brave Sea Captain* (new edition 1982) © Edward Ardizzone

Oxford University Press and the late Charles Keeping for illustrations from *Through the Window* © 1970 Charles Keeping, *The Highwayman* © 1981 Charles Keeping, *Sammy Streetsinger* © 1984 Charles Keeping

Hamish Hamilton and Raymond Briggs for illustrations from *The Snowman* © 1978 Raymond Briggs

The Bodley Head Ltd and the late Ezra Jack Keats for illustrations from *Peter's Chair* © 1968 Ezra Jack Keats; and Pat Hutchins for illustrations from *Titch* © 1971 Pat Hutchins and *You'll Soon Grow into Them, Titch* © 1983 Pat Hutchins; and Shirley Hughes for illustrations from *Up and Up* © 1979 Shirley Hughes and *Alfie Gets in First* © 1981 Shirley Hughes; and Maurice Sendak for an illustration from *Outside Over There* © 1981 Maurice Sendak

Julia MacRae Books and Gabrielle Vincent for illustrations from *Ernest and Celestine* © 1982 Gabrielle Vincent; and Anthony Browne for illustrations from *Look what I've got!* © 1980 Anthony Browne, *Hansel and Gretel* © 1981 Anthony Browne, *Gorilla* © 1983 Anthony Browne, *Willy the Wimp* © 1984 Anthony Browne, *Piggybrook* © 1986 Anthony Browne

Andersen Press Ltd and David McKee for illustrations from *Tusk Tusk* © 1978 David McKee and *Not now, Bernard* © 1980 David McKee; and Satoshi Kitamura for an illustration from *Angry Arthur* © 1982 Satoshi Kitamura

Jonathan Cape Ltd and John Burningham for illustrations from *Come away from the water, Shirley* © 1977 John Burningham and *Granpa* © 1984 John Burningham

Andre Deutsch Ltd and Ludwig Bemelmans for an illustration from *Madeline* © 1952 Ludwig Bemelmans

Angus & Robertson (UK) Ltd and Rachel Isadora for two illustrations from *Ben's Trumpet* © 1980 Rachel Isadora

E J Arnold and Martin Bailey for an illustration from *The big toe* © 1980 Martin Bailey

Octopus Books and Dick Bruna for an illustration from *The king* published by Methuen Children's Books © 1964 Dick Bruna

World's Work and Maurice Sendak for two illustrations from *Little Bear* © 1957 Maurice Sendak.